# FROM
# ZERO
## TO
# MILLIONS

INSPIRATIONAL
SUCCESS
STORIES
IN...

**NETWORK
MARKETING**

Noel Luis

FOREWORD BY: BOB PROCTOR

FROM ZERO TO MILLIONS
Inspirational Success Stories in Network Marketing
— Find Your "WHY" That Makes You Cry

ISBN: 9781650097497

Printed in the United States of America

In memory
of Ingeborg Christensen —
thanks for believing in me.

# ACKNOWLEDGMENTS

I want to personally thank you...

I dedicate this book to everyone who has had the courage and commitment to pursue their most inner desires and dreams with passion, enthusiasm, and perseverance. These people are part of the 3% who have dedicated their lives to greatness, becoming the best they can be.

By your example, you have shown the rest of us that whatever your desires, hopes, and dreams are, if you believe in yourself and have unwavering faith, determination, and commitment, your dream life will come true. I want to acknowledge my gratitude to the amazing people that I had the chance to interview and be inspired by their stories and accomplishments. Without YOU, this book would not have been written. THANK YOU.

To my mother and father for loving me unconditionally even though I didn't listen to your advice because of my stubbornness. I love you with all of my heart.

To my sister, Lene, and brother-in-law, Flemming, for being my best friends.

To Bonnie and Robert Butwin for your amazing insight into the world of network marketing.

To Art Jonak for arranging this incredible MLM cruise, creating the opportunity to meet and associate with the people in the group.

To Jordan Adler for your inspiring advice.

To Shannon Denniston for the opportunity to listen to your story, knowledge, and insights — WOW.

To Rod Cook and Marcy Cook for telling about your diverse life and life path.

To Keith McEachern for really nailing down the issue that there are no excuses. Thanks for your straightforward way of looking at things and not judging other people, but inspiring them to find their true potentials.

To Ken Seto for sharing your story; I will, from now on, always ask myself, "Who do I associate with?"

To Ken Dunn for your amazing life change — thanks for sharing. Thank you for your support and advice for publishing.

To Travis & Summer — you guys are just incredible. I have deep respect for your life journey — you absolutely deserve the best.

To Lior Skaler for really nailing down human behavior and how to inspire and empower people.

To Dakota Rea for revealing what a burning desire for improvement can do; you're a living example of making the impossible the possible. Yours was a touching story, right from your heart.

To Nikita Gromyko — your relaxed way of handling this business is endearing.

To Juan Carlos Barrios — it is such a pleasure knowing you and having the opportunity to be around you. Feeling your energy and the effect you have on people is very inspiring — thank you.

To Tom "Big Al" Schreiter for your direct guidance and humor.

To Richard for our fantastic mastermind at the beach at St. Maarten. Fantastic advice and insight into the "publishing world."

To Stephan Iscoe for your amazing and creative way of looking at marketing — thank you thousand fold for your incredible advice.

Furthermore, thanks to all you amazing people that I had the opportunity to be associated with on the MLM cruise that have supported me and introduced me to seven figure income earners and your inspiring insights: Todd and Carla Falcon, Josephine Gross, Ed and Nancy Euken, Alex W. Fraser, John Klarskov, Lyudmila Abdurakhmanova, Tom and Donna Helm, Trace, and John.

To Bob Proctor for giving me feedback and writing the foreword for this book. Further, thanks to Gina for handling all communications.

# CONTENTS

# PREFACE

What is your story? If someone made a movie out of your life, would the movie inspire people or depress them? If you think your life will inspire, continue doing what you're doing and aim for higher and higher success in life. The more successful you become, the more creative you will become, and you will inspire and help others.

If your life's movie will depress people, it's now time to think and take a hard look at yourself. Are the results in the different aspects of your life — your faith, family, friends, fitness, and finances — what you want? If not, you have 2 choices.

The first is to do NOTHING and hope and pray a miracle will happen and your life will change.

The second is to do SOMETHING, no matter how small, towards the direction of your dreams. The ironic thing is that when you pray and hope for a miracle, the miracle never comes. But when you do some-thing, no matter how small, and you take an action step everyday towards achieving your dreams, your life will become a miracle.

The stories you are about to read are stories of miracles. These stories prove that life can be lived as if everything is a miracle. Albert Einstein said that.

The stories you are about to read are inspirational stories of triumph over adversities. These stories prove that stumbling blocks can be turned into steppingstones. These stories show that successful people are the same as you and I. They have fears, they struggle, they make mistakes, and they fail too. But each time they fail, they pick themselves up, they lick their wounds, and then they try again?and again?and again?and again…until they win. Napoleon Hill said, "A quitter never wins, and a winner never quits."

But, here's a word of warning for you: once you read these inspirational stories, you will realize you HAVE NO EXCUSES for failure anymore. You will realize you are responsible for your success or failure and have no one else to blame but yourself.

If you're uneasy with the idea of taking FULL responsibility for your life, then return this book to where you bought it. This book is NOT for you.

If you are looking to blame someone else for your failures or lack of results, this book is not for you.

If you are looking for a quick fix or the next get-rich-quick scheme, then this book is NOT for you.

If you abhor working and you think that money should magically appear from the sky and fall into your lap, this book is NOT for you.

But if you're willing to do what the people interviewed in this book have done…if you're willing to do the work required, no matter what…if you're willing to spend a lot of time learning the business…if you're willing to get your hands dirty, then, by all means, read this book. Devour it. Absorb it.

All the stories you are about to read are true stories from real people, real struggles, real failures, real lives. The names in the book have not been changed. I am so grateful to have had the opportunity to interview these amazing people; I have learned so much from them and continue to grow as a person due to their enthusiasm and unwavering faith in people.

I want you to imagine that the successful people in this book are talking with you directly. Listen to their advice with your heart and engrave their advice in your mind. Then get off your behind and get to work. You must commit to work every day, even when you don't feel like doing so. If you do, you will most certainly succeed?

Dedicated to your success,

— Noel Luis

# FOREWORD

From Zero to Millions what a great title. And, in network marketing, the beautiful truth is any serious player can do it.

Noel has done a great job. With the cross-section of individuals and stories provided, there's something for everyone. And, it makes little difference where you've come from or what's happened in the past, the future is yours for the asking and the stories in this book certainly validate this point.

I don't know what your opinion of network marketing is, I can only tell you what mine was and how it has changed. For a long time, I lived with a 50 year old image of network marketing. Every time I heard the term, it would conjure up an image of a fellow going to his brother-in-law's house to pick up some soap out of his garage so that he could deliver it to the neighbor next door. The guy was probably trying to earn a couple of extra dollars, wasn't overly proud of what he was doing and was very reluctant to tell anyone that he was a distributor in network marketing. Not so today.

Today, I believe it is, without question, one of the greatest ideas to come to fruition in the history of civilization. Network marketing allows any person who is prepared to apply him or herself, to live the life that God intended us to live ? happy, healthy and wealthy ? and, most of all, grateful. I am firmly convinced network marketing is the most moral form of compensation available. There is no favoritism. There is no nepotism. There is no waste. And, there is no prejudice; anyone can become a network marketer ? and go from zero to millions.

Let me tell you how I changed my opinion. I met a man in a shopping mall who stopped and introduced himself to me and thanked me for a series of seminars I had conducted for a real estate company he was with, years back. We chatted for a few minutes and he asked me if I would meet him for lunch. He seemed like a nice guy and I agreed to meet him.

Within minutes of sitting down, it became apparent why he wanted to meet with me: he was trying to recruit me into a network marketing company. I'm pretty sure the look on my face said it all. I'd contemplated excusing myself to go to the washroom and leaving. But, as that thought entered my mind, a voice from somewhere inside of me screamed, "Coward"! At that point, the gentleman I was sitting with said, "You're not very interested in this, are you?" I told him I wasn't and proceeded to let him know that I felt he had tricked me to get me to meet him. He smiled and said, "Bob, in the material you presented in your seminar, I was especially impressed when you stated that most people criticize and ridicule ideas they don't understand." I nodded in agreement. Then he said, "Bob, do you understand network marketing?" I replied, "Of course I do." He then pushed a pen and a pad across the table and asked if I would share my perception with him. This fellow was really starting to irritate me; I could feel my blood pressure rise!

At that moment, I knew exactly what an animal must feel like when it's trapped. I was caught in my own trap and at that moment, I apologized and said, "You know, I really don't know it at all." In truth, I think when people reject network marketing, the reason they're rejecting it is because they really don't understand it.

I personally know a number of medical doctors who have to put in more time to earn less money because of the situation in which they find themselves. Many of these doctors have gone into network marketing and will be quick to tell you they have now created financial freedom for themselves. I can also point to any number of pensioners who are enjoying a wonderful retirement today because of network marketing. And, then there's the young "Generation Y" genius, Dakota Rea, with whom I've had the pleasure of working and who is featured in this book. He's waking up millions of young people to what he refers to as "The Movement" … one that aspires to help change the economy and change the world — through network marketing.

*From Zero to Millions* is a wonderful collaboration of stories and ideas that will inspire you to greatness. Realize, any success that you see someone else achieve, you can too. It all starts with a decision. Remember, it doesn't matter where you came from or what your past was like - you can change it. Start now!

  — Bob Proctor
  Featured in *The Secret* and bestselling author of *You Were Born Rich*

# CHAPTER 1

# NO EXCUSES

We had just finished lunch when I saw the "guy in the Hawaiian shirt" approaching us. I was so glad he was walking in our direction. "So you're having interviews. How is it going?" he asked with a slight smile on his face. "It's great!" I said and continued, "I want to interview you."

Only I was lying. It wasn't so great. Two BIG network marketers I had hoped to interview had just turned me down. Already feeling depressed from the rejection of these two big earners, I was pleasantly surprised when the guy in the Hawaiian shirt said I could interview him "right now."

Except he had one condition: "I want to see some sun while we do it!" Well that was easy enough. I happily followed him outside onto the deck of the cruise ship.

Unfortunately, it was a cloudy day, and there wasn't much sun. Yet a few minutes into the interview, I realized the message that can be quickly derived from Keith McEachern's story — the guy in the Hawaiian shirt

— is one as bright as the Island sun. The bright, clear message is simply this: "There are NO excuses!"

By the time you finish reading Keith's story, you will realize that whatever excuse you have used for failing in network marketing is just that — an excuse. And it is A LOUSY EXCUSE at that (the truth is all excuses are LOUSY!). And remember from the introduction that if you're good at making excuses, then you might as well close this book and return it right now. This book is NOT for you. But if you take responsibility for your life, by all means read this chapter, be inspired, and learn from Keith's story.

## Keith's Darkest Secret

"I built my network marketing business from prison," Keith said matter-of-factly. My jaw dropped and I was speechless. I was not expecting anything like this. He proceeded, "I was a former marijuana smuggler. The truth is that it was never really about the money. I met this Caribbean girl and we developed a relationship. She wanted to smuggle marijuana and since we had become close, I began to help her."

Keith continued with some embarrassment in his voice. Then he explained, "But I realized the error of my ways and that I had drifted down a wrong path." In order to get things turned around, he separated from this girl and the business and set out on a new path. A short time had passed when he began dating a young lady who would help contribute new purpose and direction to his life: that of a husband, a father to their son, and an extremely successful network marketer.

Early in their dating relationship, Keith shared the details of his past life with his soon-to-be wife. Having put the past behind, they spent the next few years building their lives and a family together. They were married, enjoyed the birth of a son, and were in the process of building a dream home in a secluded, beautiful setting. Life was progressing nicely when his past unexpectedly came crashing back into the present.

Seven years after being completely removed from the marijuana smuggling business, the federal government made an abrupt and unannounced visit to his home, and by no means was it a house warming. Keith was handcuffed and hauled away on the spot. In an instant, his new life was turned upside down and inside out. His freedom and all his possessions were about to disappear.

Keith explained that upon sentencing, "I found out from the judge that I had 24 days to set my life in order prior to me going to prison." Ironically enough, during such a challenging time, there was a bright spot. The co-founders of a new-to-launch network marketing company had asked Keith to be the very first distributor. At the time, all the company knew was that it wanted to be in nutrition, yet it didn't even have its first product. Virtually all they had was a name. Basically all that Keith had was 24 days, a vision, a passion, and — most importantly — a "why" and, for Keith, that was enough to go to work.

"So I called 1,500 people before going to prison. I spent 20-hour days, I looked like shit afterwards, and I told my wife 'Honey, don't worry about me. I will get enough rest in prison,'" he said with a chuckle. I laughed.

Then his face looked serious. "You have to have a 'why' that makes you cry," he said. "And my 'why' was I didn't want to see my wife and kids go hungry." And this "why" propelled him to do what many would find impossible. In those 24 days before he went to prison, he managed to recruit 44 people in his down-line without any marketing materials, before websites, and without a single product.

Recruiting 44 people was a great start, but he knew it would still take effort on his part for it to continue, and he wasn't about to let prison slow him down. Keith found one most creative way to support his down-line and continue to grow his business from behind bars.

## The Phone Room

"One of the things I've learned is the importance of knowing what is valuable to people. I realized that the warden we had at the time measured how good his prison was being run by how clean it was kept," Keith explained. One of the "eye sores" or problem areas in prison was the phone room. The inmates and prisoners would throw their trash everywhere. They would stick their gum on the walls and throw it on the floor. It was a mess.

Keith was pretty handy, had a strong work ethic, and was never afraid of getting his hands dirty, so he volunteered to clean the phone room. He promised the warden he would have one of the cleanest phone rooms a prison could have if only he would secure for Keith some uninterrupted time each day to maintain it.

He began by stripping the floor bare and then put on several layers of wax and buffed it in between. The initial process took him a long time to do but in the long run, the benefits were clear. Now the floors were much easier to keep clean. The gum and trash and scuff marks would come off much more easily. Prior to rejuvenating the floors, it would take a good four hours to clean. After that, it only took one hour. Of course, he neglected to tell anyone else about this time savings. He then conveniently had 3 hours a day of alone time in the phone room.

So while it was legal for an inmate to use the telephone to make personal calls, business calls were strictly prohibited. Nonetheless, Keith risked being caught. He used his time in the phone room to call prospects, conduct 3-way calls with his up-line, and call his wife to handle the paperwork to close the deals. Slowly but surely, he built his down-line. His why was so strong that he risked getting found out and being thrown in the "hole." He was eventually found out and got thrown in the hole, but Keith did it again and again.

So the next time you think you have no time or it's no fun to call prospects, remember Keith's "The Phone Room" story.

Keith told me one thing I will never forget: "The real measure of a person is the degree to which he takes full responsibility."

And for Keith, this is not just some empty slogan. He never used excuses to deter his efforts. How easy would it have been for Keith to give up behind bars? How much do we take for granted, even the simple act of making a phone call, or in today's world, sending a text or an email? In prison, Keith faced a completely different reality and, despite these limitations, he pushed on and persevered when most people would have just quit.

The warden eventually saw that Keith was different from the other prisoners. He was handy and very responsible. In 13 months, Keith received a transfer to a work cadre where he once again helped improve and renovate, this time historical buildings in federal parks. Due to that good work, seven months later, the warden decided to transfer him to a halfway house.

As luck would have it, there was no halfway house available, so they allowed Keith to stay in his own house under a home confinement sentence. This was, of course, the ideal situation since it gave him even more time to spend on his now growing network marketing business. Incredibly enough, after being in prison 26 months, Keith had built a network marketing organization that provided him a whopping $20,000 a month in passive income, and this was back in the 80s!

"After I came out of prison, I worked like a mad man. My income grew from $20,000 a month to $250,000 a month in just a few years," Keith said with a big smile on his face. My jaw dropped again. This time it dropped not out of shock but out of admiration. This unassuming man in a Hawaiian shirt makes more money than 97% of the people on the planet, and you would never have guessed it by the way he carries himself, by the way he speaks, and definitely not by his Hawaiian shirt.

## "Saddling Up"

I asked Keith this question: "Why do most people who join network marketing fail while a few people like you succeed?" His answer is so true, and the way he answered it will make me remember his answer forever. He told me that before you ride a horse, typically people start by putting a saddle on the horse's back. In network marketing, "too many people are always 'saddling up.' They will put the saddle on, and they will say 'Hmm…it's not that sunny today, so I will not ride the horse. Maybe tomorrow I will.'

"When tomorrow comes, they will saddle up again and maybe even sit on the horse, but they will say 'Hmm…maybe the trail is not clear, so I will clear the trail first before riding the horse.' And when that is done, by tomorrow, they will saddle up again and will have yet another excuse.'

"Most people are always just 'saddling up,' and they don't dare just ride the horse," Keith explained. "Take it one step further and, if you look at history, there were cultures who were extremely skilled riders even before the saddle existed. Most people are always getting ready. You don't have to know everything there is to know in order to do it (the business). You just have to believe that you can do it." These are powerful words from a man who acts in a massive way whether or not the "saddle is ready."

## Keith's 2nd & 3rd Best Ways to Generate Prospects

I asked him, "Keith, what are ways for you to generate leads?" He began by sharing something interesting. "I don't recruit family and friends. Most network marketers say that you should start with family and friends, but it does not work. To this day, I have best friends and family members who have seen all the millions of dollars I've made and still scoff at the business."

## Making a List

He continued, "You want to start first with people in your community whom you have done business with in the past. Start with your real estate agent, your barber, your plumber. Anyone whom you have paid for a service is someone who might be open to a network marketing opportunity."

## The 3-ft. Circle

"I am also good with the 3-ft. circle," Keith continued. "Most of these so-called network marketing 'experts' will tell you DO NOT prejudge people as to for whom the business is suited. I say you cannot NOT prejudge. In fact, you should use your intuition to help you avoid engaging those whom you know just won't work the business." Keith is so different from the mold, and his results attest to that.

Keith went on to explain that he looks for those people with "attitude" or those with personality. He looks for that bagger at the grocery store who times himself and tries to beat his fastest time to bag groceries. He looks for people who dare to be different, and then he asks them a provocative question after he establishes some rapport with them which is, "When is it that you are going to become the person you are meant to be?"

He makes people understand they have unrealized potential, and this makes them feel good. This is when he will then ask the question, "Have you found an opportunity that has given you everything you've ever wanted in life and made your life an absolute dream, or are you still open-minded?" When people say they are open-minded, then Keith uses this question as a perfect transition to introduce them to his network marketing opportunity.

## The Bulletin Board

While making a list of people you've done business with and befriending people in your 3-ft. circle sounds great, nothing will compare with the power of a simple lead generation technique that Keith has perfected over the years. I call it "the Bulletin Board Technique," Keith said jokingly.

"When you go to a barber shop, a restaurant, or even a church, and you see a bulletin board where small business owners can post their adver-tisement and business card, and it's neatly organized, there's a good chance that I've cleaned it and organized it. I clean up half the bulletin boards in all of America." Keith laughed at his own joke. And I smiled, but the confusion on my face must have been apparent, because Keith explained what he meant.

"On the bulletin boards, small business owners post their ads and business cards. They're doing marketing, so they're selling something. I collect their names and phone numbers and I call them. I tell them, 'I am building a multi-million dollar business, and I am building a massive sales organization in your area.'"

Just mentioning this prompts the prospects to ask him, "What do you do?" This, in turn, becomes a good segue for Keith to talk about his MLM business.

The Bulletin Board technique turned out to be very profitable for Keith — so much so that when I asked him what would he do differently to his network marketing business if he can do it all over again he said, "I would start using the bulletin board clean up technique much sooner."

## How to Make $100,000 per Phone Call?

"There was this colleague of mine," Keith slowly explained, "and I really wanted him to be part of my team." But each time they spoke, the colleague gave every reason and excuse not to join: why Keith's company would fail, and how his company was the much better opportunity.

As it turned out, this colleague's company wasn't all it was cracked up to be and, as a result, this colleague began to struggle financially. In fact, it got to the point that he did not even have the money to pay for his house. And so it happened that after 9 years and 27 calls, it was time. It was time for this colleague to confess financial problems, and Keith volunteered to help him with his lodging issues. And it was finally time for this colleague to join Keith's team. And what a decision it turned out to be for both the colleague and Keith.

For over the next two years, this colleague built an organization which has made Keith more than $2.7 million and growing! Given that Keith made 27 phone calls, he estimates those calls were worth well over $100,000 per phone call.

Next time you're afraid of following up with your prospects, think about this story and the potential value lost simply by not making that phone call!

## *What if The 1,101st Phone Call Is a "YES!"?*

I asked Keith, "How do you keep yourself motivated?" I explained that some network marketers, especially beginners, get discouraged easily with rejection, or even the fear of rejection, and a lot of them give up too early. Keith said, "Dry spells are natural. In one case I made 1,100 presentations and all of them said NO. And that was after I had already achieved significant success."

He further explained how one time he had gotten a list of 1,800 people, and he called 1,100 of them. One by one, all of these 1,100 people said NO to his sales presentation. Instead of getting discouraged, he figured since he has made successful sales presentations before, the problem was THEM not him. His strong self-belief carried him through this long "dry spell," and his 1,101st presentation turned into a sale.

What about you? How much do you believe in you?

# FROM ZERO TO MILLIONS STRATEGY

· There are No Excuses!
· When you saddle up, don't forget to "ride the horse."
· Find your "WHY" that makes you cry.
· Clean up bulletin boards in your travels.
· Don't take rejection personally.
· Intuition is important.
· Prejudging people is not always wrong if it leads to people with the right attitudes.
· Take action regardless of your circumstances.

# CHAPTER 2

# THE MOVEMENT

All right, Dakota, tell us your story. How did you get into Network Marketing?

---

Well, I usually tell people that ask me about my story that it will take one hour and a cup of coffee because it is a long one. I have thought many times of writing a book because people like love stories, and this is truly a love story.

When I was sixteen, I was really struggling. I was hanging out with the wrong people. Who knows — it might have been the right people because they led me to the point where I am now, but I had the risk of going down the wrong path. Everyone has that fork in the road.

I started out as a quarterback of my high school football team, but messed that up. Because I decided to party instead, I chose to be around those types of people that just weren't making the best decisions they could make. I was getting distracted trying to be the life of the party and was always getting into trouble. This seems to be a common problem these days. But what I am about to share is going to give a lot of hope to those in our profession.

One thing that really made me pay attention to what I was doing was having a mentor. I would stop and consider, "What would they think of me?"

Even if they were not looking, I would wonder what they thought of what I was doing because I admired these people so much. I actually started to change because no matter if they were looking or not, I wanted to feel good about myself when I looked them in the eyes. I would ask myself, "Am I the best person I can be?"

I met a girl from Holland at a Christmas party right after I finished boarding school where I had gotten into all these troubles. I was basically away from my family for three months, and I broke down emotionally. I had to go through this to find out who I really was inside.

When I met this girl, I was enchanted. She was from Europe and had beautiful blonde hair and blue eyes, and I was captivated by her French accent. She actually wrote a number on my hand. I did not realize it at the time, but that number that she wrote on my hand that Christmas evening would lead to this industry, Network Marketing. I would like to change that term to personal development with a pay plan attached, because that is what it truly embodies.

I was with her for nine months. She was the first girl I fell in love with, and she decided to go back to Europe to visit her family because she was a foreign student, living with her mom in the United States temporarily. Having never traveled before, I asked to go with her.

So off I went with her to Europe for my first time with my very first passport. At the time, I had long hair, baggy jeans, and looked like the cool guy from down the street. Unfortunately, I figured out quickly that her dad did not like me very much. He was having secret meetings with her at dinner behind my back, trying to convince her that she needed to stay there for her younger brother and sister and make me go home to America alone.

These secret meetings with her father kept happening again and again, but we were two young love birds traveling in Europe together with beautiful windmills as a backdrop. We were finally invited to have lunch together with her father, but he brought two really, really big Dutch body builders with him. This did not bode well for me.

So, eventually one night in the house in Holland, in a small town, the sun was setting on the beach, I hit my breaking point. I could not take it any more. I asked her, "Ona, are you going to go home with me or are you going to stay with your family?" She answered sadly that her dad made her choose between me and her younger brother and sister. What a hard choice. So she decided to stay.

I started running. Here I was in this small town in Europe by myself, tears gushing from my eyes. This was when I realized what it felt like to have a broken heart.

To my surprise, she ended up calling me on this phone at her grandma's house, following me with bags, and promising, "I will never leave you again." I thought it was going to be a good ending. But when we got back to the United States, her parents said that we could never see each other again. No happy ending there.

Imagine being in love with someone, your first love, and in the peak of your relationship, all of a sudden you get ripped away from each other. I felt like my heart was being ripped in two. I only had two weeks left before she had to go back to Europe, and I would never see her again. What I didn't know at the time was that it was a blessing in disguise.

So what did I learn from all of this? There was a silver lining to be found. This difficult situation where I had my heart broken in two made me ask myself, "What do I need to change about myself as a young person?"

I think there are so many millions of young people out there that just don't have that self-awareness because they haven't hit the bottom yet. They haven't lost something that they care about so much that they start to look at themselves and say, "How can I be a better person? How can I become a man?" What is that transition?

In my opinion, Network Marketing is the answer. Because it's personal development with a pay plan attached. Financial freedom leads to time freedom. Without money, you can't pay the bills, you're forced to work, and in many cases families choose to place their children in day care. They have other people raise their children.

What we're effectively talking about here is that maybe we can create a movement where we influence these young people to go on the journey of personal development like I did, where they look at themselves and ask, "How can I become a better person, a better business person, a better man?" That's the key.

Let's go back to my story, though. As her parents had doomed us to separation, I had to watch my first love fly away on an airplane, probably never to see her again. But I told her parents, "I don't care what it takes; I'm going to make it happen. I'm going to go to college. I'm going to get a degree in International Business."

I went to an Intercontinental University so that I could travel and have professors abroad. I did anything and everything it took to make sure I could go to school in her country. I kept telling myself that I would go to college and get a good degree. I would get rich enough to have a home in Holland where she lived and have a home back in my country. Her parents looked at me and said, "Oh, yeah — yeah, right." Right? They challenged me.

I got the most important thing in my life taken away from me, and they challenged me and said I couldn't have her ever again. They even said I could never do anything about it. But what did I do? I fought for it. But, I fought with emotion so powerful, the emotion of love.

With the three most powerful emotions that Napoleon Hill talks about in *Think and Grow Rich*, I felt there was nothing that could stop me. If you use your heart rather than your brain, you can actually become very powerful. This power will help you think about the outcomes much better and will keep you going, no matter how hard it gets. It will drive you to go make that next phone call.

So, I quit all the bad friends I had accumulated — they were gone from my life. I was by myself with my head down. I was a grim, grumpy, depressed, sad person. Several months went by, and it was the worst time in my life. We had broken up over the phone and even though I was down, I was still determined. I was going back to Europe to see her again, and I was going to make enough money to do it. Sadly enough, even after I made all that money, I never saw my true love again. I had a broken heart, truly. But despite that, I found deep comfort in my faith in God, my mentors, and the vision I had for my life.

There is a saying that money isn't everything, but it sure does pay for the trip. Money doesn't buy you love, but it sure does pay for the trip, right?

After I began to look at myself and evaluate what I needed to improve, I figured that I would need money. After speaking to young generation Y people, I realized that colleges and universities are big businesses. In the same way, the college loan industry was a big business. Did you know that only 1 in 10 college students actually use their degree? The sad part is that the average college student has roughly $40 to $100 thousand dollars in debt.

What are we doing as a nation, as a worldwide nation, putting our young people in debt and taking advantage of them? How are we going to ever survive in this economy? How are we going to ever get over this debt problem or, rather, debt challenge? I like to use the word "challenge" because a problem is a problem, but a challenge is something that you can overcome. So how can we get over this unless we unite the generations? We'll touch on this more as my story continues.

I was sitting at my sister's house one night and she was talking with a friend who was sharing a story about her father. She said she had asked her dad for $20, and he gave her a $100 bill. When she asked him why, he said, "because we are never going to have to worry about money again." They had just started a new business, and I nearly lost my head with wondering, "Is this possible?" I was looking for anything and everything that would get me to my goal of financial security.

I have said that you can have the best leaders in the world, but if they are not ready in their hearts, they are not ready. They are not ready to become who they are meant to be. They might be a leader and have a leader inside of them, but they are not ready to put it into action until they are REALLY ready in their heart.

That day I was ready. It was September 16, 2004. It is funny how you remember those days. I went into that opportunity meeting, and crossed the street. I walked over and everybody thought I was this young kid with long hair, baggy jeans, and just there for the appetizers. No one thought a young kid was going to go to a meeting and be a business person and, because of this, no one was talking to me. I got to hear all these unsolicited testimonials from all these people who were getting checks every week. No one was trying to sell me, but I was listening.

So when no one was paying attention, I went over to the top leader, grabbed him and said, "Listen, man, what is this and can I make money with it? I will do anything." Imagine, I will do anything, right? So he started drawing circles on the board: "This is you, this is Bill, and this Mary." I didn't understand and asked, "Who the heck are Bill and Mary? I don't know Bill and Mary." I just said, "Can I make a little bit of money at this?" And he said, "Yes."

So I got in at age 17, with an $800 package. I found the way to get that much at least. My dad was skeptical and thought it looked like Amway, but my dad has always supported me. He is a great guy. His friend expressed concern as well, but I didn't care. I was going to do it no matter what because I never, at that point, had found something that could actually create that amount of income and time freedom, financial freedom, with sweat equity — your own work.

Because I was young kid, I was not rich. I did not have a bank to go to that would lend a 17-year-old kid a million dollars. Many young people today have the same restraints. This is why network marketing is the perfect vehicle for young people if they want to be successful. I do not know of any other business that you can start with such a low start-up fee. With hard work and determination, I had recruited 18 people personally within the first three weeks.

I had so much enthusiasm on fire. There is a saying that "enthusiasm on fire is better than knowledge on ice."

When I met with people to recruit, I would often tear up when I told them my story. My passion and drive just could not stay under wraps. Some in our line of work joke that they cannot sign up their brother-in-laws, but I had my brother-in-law pulling out $1600 cash, $800 for him and $800 for my sister, because both signed up for the opportunity. I convinced anybody and everybody because they saw the passion in my eyes.

Because of this enthusiasm and passion, my business started to explode. I remember looking at my organization and every time I pressed the refresh button, my team was growing. Can you imagine that?

I literally didn't have any idea what was happening. So, all of a sudden, I have a team in 20 different states from our kitchen table in Oregon — a team from 20 different states!

Life was changing quickly. I remember flying out first class when I was 19 years old, staying at the Hyatt, playing on a Jack Nicholas golf course, and getting picked up at the airport by a leader of mine that I had not met before. Here I was, a young kid who had started from my kitchen table and went all the way across the country to speak in Orlando. Man, was I in for something, right? Everybody started calling me the young superstar in the company and I said, "What? What did I do?" I got this fancy new car. People asked what I was doing. It was time for a revelation.

I was sitting at a coffee shop outside on the internet checking the volume of my down-line. All of a sudden, a friend of mine from high school, Brandon, came up. He said, "Hey, man! How is it going? I haven't seen you in a long time." And he said, "My mom saw you on a flight back home. She said you were just at a business meeting, and you gave her your card. And she said you were in some internet business. And, hey man, I've seen you drive around in this nice car. What are you doing?" And all of a sudden, without any hesitation, he signed up. I think that is what a leader really is; you'll recognize a leader when they come along. They'll simply say, "That's what you're doing? I'm in." They understand. They're decision-makers.

So he got in. And every single day, without hesitation, he would send a text message to me asking me when and where we were meeting, often at a coffee shop. We would always have our meetings going on with the older generations. There were people twice my age, and I was actually teaching them! But I still wanted the younger generation too; I wanted both. So we started right on to the houses of young generation Y people, meeting in their garages if need be.

Then we started filling up coffee shops. We met at a coffee shop every day and, pretty soon, our group got so big that the coffee shop was getting overflowed. And all of a sudden we carried these paper applications with us to see who could sign up the most people and get them to join our group, our movement. Some of the young people started signing up the people behind the counter of the coffee shop so the managers would kick us out. They were all 19 years old. We were having fun, but I learned that a lot of the young people looked to me for guidance; I could see it in their eyes.

I was only drinking coffee. I stopped drinking alcohol at that time for health reasons. I wasn't 21 yet, and I wanted to be the best person I could be. I began to notice that all these young people who were getting into trouble doing drugs and alcohol stopped because I was not doing it. They said they realized that none of them were drinking at one of the clubs they frequented. They told me, "You know what, you've really helped changed my whole outlook on life."

And I've seen a lot of these young people since then; they still have that mindset. And the mindset will always stay with them. No matter if they succeed in network marketing or not, they're going to have that mindset. And as Jim Rohn said, "Your personal philosophy will be the determining factor of how your life turns out."

I'm 24 now. And generation Y, if many Pulitzers don't know it, is the generation that is the sons and the daughters of the baby boomers, which is the largest generation in the history of the world. They were born after the World War II generation. They started the trends. They were so big! Supply beats demands. Ever see this in Business 101?

The amount of people that are in the world creates an amount of demand. If there are 72 million people in the United States, that's 72 million people who need to eat. So you could sell 72 million hamburgers every single day. But if there are only 8 million people, that's only 8 million hamburgers you can sell every day, right?

When the baby boomers had sons and daughters, what happens again — this bigger generation has another one? I go around the world now and ask, "How many of you are baby boomers? How many of you have more than one child at home?" Most of them raise their hands. So families are getting bigger. Now there are about 80 million generation Y individuals around ages 20 to 33 in the United States.

The baby boomers started network marketing. They started Amway. They started Herbalife. They started Avon, which is over a hundred-year-old company. They really started this whole movement when they were younger, near the end of the Vietnam War. They created a movement with Martin Luther King to make us all one, together, and equal. Equality. He had a dream, right? There were many movements that sprung out of that philosophy.

More recently, generation Y helped elect the first African-American president of the United States, Barack Obama. Whether I agree with him or not, I'm not saying. I do not talk about politics or religion because I don't want people to think of me any differently, because I accept anybody and everybody. In this business, we accept anybody and everybody because we're an international business, plus it's just a lot about who we are. We grow and learn from each other, no matter where we come from, how old we are, or how we look. Race doesn't matter. We all need to work together to help each other grow and start a movement to become better people. And that's what it's all about.

Personal development with a pay plan attached. What this is all leading up to is that for the last seven years, I've been on a mission. Ever since I looked in the eyes of my friends, my comrades, when I was building the business with them, I've built many down-lines in 28 countries all over the world in the last seven years. I've invested in people.

And I don't say that to impress anybody. I just say it to impress upon them that I've been there. And I've seen it. And I'm still going. I still have 7,000 tracks of personal development on my iPod. I love listening. I go to Barnes & Noble like a kid in a candy store. I seriously got so excited when my good friend, Jordan Adler, handed me a great book called *Beach Money* in the training, which I recommend everybody read.

I said, "Great! This is like candy!" It is great because this is what has helped change my life. There are so many great books out there by Jim Rohn, Brian Tracy, Dennis Swancy, and Napoleon Hill, who happens to be one of my heroes. This is why I wanted to help the world.

If you take a look at our economy these days, you see a lot of people with negative speculations. CNN, which we call "constant negative news" makes everyone wonder, "Oh no! What's happening? The world! What's going to happen?"

And I really feel that the Chinese proverb that says in every failure, there's an opportunity truly applies. I see that something big is coming, and it may lead to yet another movement. The baby boomers like Jef

Welsh, Jordan Adler, Art Jonak, Dave Galder, and Big Al Shreiter are echoing this sentiment that the next movement is about to come.

This is exciting for me because for the last seven years, I have been writing a book, Gen Y, The New Baby Boomers in Network Marketing with Art Jonak, and it's a home study course. I've been in the magazines like Networking Times— look for the January/February issue 2008 with the "Generation Y" front cover, Network Marketing Business Journal Network Marketing Magazine. To give you an idea of how big this generation Y is, they total 8 million more than the baby boomer generation who started it all. They started Coca-Cola, Gerber, Avon, all these Fortune 500 companies. Now we're coming together, this next movement, a big moment. We have two big booming generations with generation X in the middle, and, all combined, that's the biggest group of unified generations in history!

So, the next companies, the next big companies, are going to be phenomenally large. I predict they will be a $20 billion company or more. And that's not the major mission here. The major mission is to help all these younger people who are going out of these education systems and asking, "Okay, what do I do now?" They're so lost. There's a book called The Lost Generation There are 500 million Generation Y people in India. That's half a billion people, half their population. In addition, there are more generation Y people in China than the entire population of the Unites States.

I was in that meeting and I saw maybe a few people in their 20's, and they're generation Y. Then I decided I will never go on this cruise again without bringing on a large group of young people. I will never go to these events again unless there's a large group of young people with me.

I want to say, "What can I do?" I've been building large teams. We just built a team in Europe, together with some good friends of mine, that is a multi-million dollar down-line. It's averaging just 27, 28 years old, and some started to see. Any companies consulting with them to generate new programs, like Avon did with the "Meet Mark" program, created a program just for generation Y. They didn't change what Avon had.

They created a separate branded one. It had taken Avon over a hundred years to get to $5 billion annually. As soon as they launched the Avon Mark Program separately, they went from $5 billion to $8 billion in one year. That's a $3 billion dollar increase. That's half of their total sales in a hundred years in ONE YEAR!

They looked at mothers and daughters, realized they don't like the same things — the same music, the same cars. So they created different brands to bridge that gap; it's Business 101 if you think about it. Now Avon is the largest direct selling company in the whole world. It boggles my mind to see all these other network marketing companies that are so stuck in the past.

They're so old school. It's surprising how many CEO's I've sat down with. I was one of the youngest and first one of the people to be flown out to Trump Tower in Manhattan to meet Donald Trump. Then I had the opportunity to hang out with Todd Stanley, who is a great guy, by the way, and visit his Massachusetts office where we talked about this big vision, and I've been to many other companies. And it just didn't sink in.

Then I said to myself, "Gosh! If no one's going to do this, I've got to do it myself." What's that saying? "If you want something done right, you've got to do it yourself."

And I'm so passionate about this profession of network marketing and direct sales because it's changed my life. When I first got a personal development book in my hand, that's what led me to this cruise.

Hearing Art Jonak's voice from a CD program called *The Simple Art of Duplication*, I heard his voice, and thought, "That Art Jonak guy seems like a really cool guy." And then I found out about the MLM Cruise. I came out 6 years ago and I haven't missed one in 6 years. And I don't plan on missing any.

I'm going to keep bringing in a lot of young people here because these are the people that have changed my mind, changed my life, and continue to change my life as I grow. How dare we hide this from the young generation? They're going out of college. They're in debt. They are living with their friends, their family, and they have no hope. The suicide rates continue to rise.

If they had a vision or something that they could be excited about or a group of positive people that they could hang out with who would pat them on the back, maybe that would be the one thing that would keep them going. Keep them striving to be better people. This hope has the possibility to save the world and the economy. It's from the ground up that we can come together and can help one another.

So we're creating a movement. That's what we all want in the United States. We're creating a movement — of our generation. All of us must come together to help unite the generations. It is only then that Generation Y, the Baby Boomers, and Generation X will come together and will help change the world. They'll help spread marketing and personal growth around the world. And we can all come together as one. It is said that he who unites the generations shall be blessed. And if we all do that together, we can save millions of young people's lives.

Not only that, but we need mentors to come together with us and say, "you can do it!" because we look up to them. And the young people will bring energy and excitement. When you look at them, everyone will say, "This is fun! This is a fun business!" This is how it should be; this business is supposed to be fun.

We're creating a movement that aspires to help change the economy, change the world, and help create more peace on earth because you don't want to ever mess with your down-line. Network marketing is in over a hundred countries around the world now, which is exciting.

So we all have a plan. Next year on the cruise we're going to have my friend Lior Skaler and 50 young leaders from Canada. I have an aspiration of younger leaders from around the world. We want to make sure we get as many leaders as possible from all the countries. We don't want to leave anybody out. I feel a bit like Napoleon Bonaparte, leading a revolution, saying, "Let's go!" And then, "I can't do it alone."

I'm talking to you! I can't do it alone. So we all need to unite together. We all need to come together and stop looking down on one another. Stop fighting with one another and say, "Hey, you can do it!" And that's what network marketing does.

If we're attached to each other's success, of course we're going to want each other to succeed, but it's more than that. Let's just help each other out. But I mean generation Y right now, I'm telling you — Avon already saw the fastest growing sales in their whole entire company's history.

For us to come together in this industry and create these brands for generation Y, and baby boomers to come together like Avon did, the number one direct selling company in the entire world, success leaves footprints. You better follow the best you know, follow where the money is. I'll say it again. Follow where the money is. Follow where the people are. And the movements are the trends. We're creating a movement.

I am going to start writing a lot of articles about movement in all of the networking magazines. And we are going to make this known so that we can all come together and save a lot of young people's lives. And we can get a lot of young people, as well as older people, and their parents too. We'll create a big movement together and, like Art Jonak says, "Rising Tide," "Let's All Shift," and "Mastermind Event," which I recommend everybody going to as well. We're going to bring a lot of young people to that because we want to put it in their mindset that if a troubled young kid with long hair and baggy pants from Oregon can be on a cruise in middle of the Caribbean talking to you great people, and talking about movements, I mean, man — I love it! I love this business. And out there, we're not sure with the world. That's the Movement.

## It's about the movement .. and the money

It's about both. There are a lot of people who'd say it's not about the money, but I think that's about their programming that they are not good enough to have it. Money to me is just to pay for privilege. It's not a bad thing. Money is a good thing. It's just a piece of paper that says, "Okay, we've added value to the market place," as Jim Rohn says. You must add value; people are not going to give you money unless your service or products helps them out, right?

Imagine you're playing football, you're the quarterback, and you throw for the touchdown. Your receiver will be thinking, "I've got to catch this." And he's going to have to get past the 250-pounders. There's going to be a lot of people tying to stop him from getting in the end zone. So that's your reward. That's your score. You put it on the board. It is the same with your business. You may have many obstacles along the way, but it sure feels great to have someone say, "This product helped me with my life." It's almost like scoring a touchdown!

People need money to live. Otherwise, what would happen? They just couldn't survive. They need water. Water costs money. So it's just a circulation of currency. That's where the economy starts. That's how people get into action. So to me, the money is a part of it. It's the point that Napoleon Hill talks about. There are 12 areas of success. Not just money, but harmony, human relations, and sound physical health are all areas of success. But it's much more than financial security; it's all of it working together.

So this is about living the best life you can on this earth. When we are on the islands together in the middle of the Caribbean, we always say to everybody, "Oh! Tough life" in a sarcastic way. But man, isn't it amazing to come on a ship? It's like we're all one big family. So to me it's more than just the money, of course. But the money is a big part of it. It's about helping all of us come together and say, "Wow!" I call it "transformed," because it's proven that everything is energy. Einstein's formula, $E = MC^2$, shows that energy never dies. It's also a scientific fact.

So, where do we go after this? Nobody knows. But we know that the time we have on this earth is limited, so let's make the best of it. You can have all the money in the world, but unless you have your friends to share it with, you have nothing. There's a saying that it's better to be on the beach with the person that you love than in a mansion by yourself. I would like to amend that a bit by saying it's better to be in a mansion with the person you love if the mansion is by the beach! So, then you have both. Network marketing is like that — it allows you to imagine a life where anything is possible.

## The mindset for success

What is the attitude that is responsible for success, if I were to boil it down to a few things? I think, above all, that it's faith — faith in God, faith in yourself, and faith in the people around you. And whatever God you represent, that's fine. That's great. I believe in God and when I was young kid, I was praying. I started praying again, all of a sudden, when my life started to change. When I had faith in something bigger than myself — God, mentors — I started to say, "What would they think of me if I were not the best person I could be?"

That got me to move away from the things that were holding me back. And so, it's faith. It's really faith in everything you do because that keeps you going. If you don't have the vision and the hope and the faith, then you have nothing to look forward to. So that's what it is for me: faith, belief, and trust (FBT).

The subject of trust brings to mind a time that I was in Singapore, and I met this billionaire who was from my own state. I asked him for his advice, and he said, "Read this book, the *Speed of Trust* by Stephen Covey's son." And what it talks about is that a business organization never moves or grows faster than the level of the speed of trust. So, if it's a high level of trust, it moves as fast as a startled cat. I thought that was funny. If you have a lot of trust in the people around you, and they trust in you, people just move. I think faith is the number one belief.

Number two, trust in God, in yourself, and everybody you work with. And surround yourself with people that you trust. Keep your integrity at all times. Just remember that we're all not perfect. If you're thinking to yourself, "Gosh, I'm not a perfect person," just remember that you are human and this is a journey. Also, keep in mind the saying by Helen Keller that "life is either a daring adventure or it's nothing at all."

How can you have the good without the dark side? How can you have light without dark? There's a contrast. Of course, we're on the good side. We're on the loving side, the personal development side, the success side. It's a daring adventure! Life is not going to be perfect. But the definition of integrity is doing the right thing especially when no one is looking. What you do when you're behind closed doors?

I remember when I was in ROTC, I was in the bathroom. As I was leaving the bathroom, one of the sergeants walked in and asked, "What are you doing?"

I said, "What do you mean, 'What am I doing'?"

"What's that towel doing on the ground?"

I said, "I didn't put that towel on the ground."

He said, "It doesn't matter if you're the one who put that towel on the ground or not. What matters is that if no one was in the room, and you had the self-discipline to reach down and pick that towel up and put it in the trash can, you have self-discipline, which I also attribute to integrity."

Strong words! So what are you doing when no one else is looking? Because I think that will be well-represented in magnetism when you go out in the world and you meet people. They can sense that energy in you, that you did the right thing. And you're constantly improving. Don't knock yourself down, because controlling your mind is a very hard thing. We've all been through tough times. Conditioning your mind takes practice. You can't just say, "Oh, I'm a perfect person. I don't do anything wrong. I'm destined for greatness." Well, gosh, how can you make a touch down without running through all the tackles and dodging all the hurdles? Jumping and falling, and getting bruised. We're not perfect.

Don't ever beat yourself up because you were brought on this earth that way. We all go through these trials, tribulations, and we're all going to be transformed and be who-knows-where. So, you have two choices: you can either live your whole life with your head down, complaining about where you are, or you can do whatever it takes to be as happy as you can be at that moment. I'm going to be around my friends who believe in me, and that's network marketing.

That's a Movement. That's what it's all about. We're all together as imperfect human beings. We're humans called human beings, not human doings, right? So we need those "human being" times to realize that we're not perfect. We're here to grow, to learn together and only then can we do the things that we're supposed to do together.

## Cutting down the learning curve

The learning curve is always a challenge for everyone new to any business. If I could do things differently, I would keep my friendships strong.

Jim Rohn, one of my heroes, said, "You can always make more money." But what matters most are the people in your life in your skill set. You can always make more money. It will always be there. It's your contacts, your reputation, and the friends you know in high influence that help you get back on your feet. Because, if you're good friends with Oprah, for example, and you lost everything, you would only have to make one phone call, right?

One phone call. So how influential are your friends? That's one of the things that changed in my life. I had all these friends that were calling me asking what I was doing, what books I was reading, where I was traveling. I do the same thing with my contacts — it's all about building relationship. I call my good friends like Tom Big Al Schreiter, Art Jonak, Jef Welsh, Jordan Adler, Nikita Gromyko, and all these other amazing individuals that I've met along the way. I make a point to keep in contact with them on a business and social level because I know that when you keep your relationships strong, they will be there for you when you fail.

I have a philosophy that I've had to learn and I'm still getting better at it: "Either they're your friend or they're your friend and business partner." This philosophy makes you never attach to a prospect. If you think of each new prospect as a new friend and business partner, and they end up not doing business with you, at least you have a new friend, and you can never have enough friends. Who doesn't want more friends on Facebook?

I think it's better to have friends like these people on this Caribbean cruise or anywhere you go in the world. With that security, you can travel anywhere and you have a place to stay, you are welcome, because you have friends everywhere. It's an international business, and that is why I would keep my friendships strong.

## Where to begin

As a beginner, as a newbie network marketer, what are the top three skills to develop in order to be successful? I would say that it goes back to the faith, belief, and trust because the skills will come if you have enough of these three pillars of success.

When I first started at age seventeen, I didn't have any skills, but I still signed up eighteen people in my first three weeks. That was not just skills at play. That was pure emotion, enthusiasm, passion of faith, belief, and trust. I would do anything it took, and I still will.

The willpower kept me in because, as Jim Rohn says, "You'll either see me on the top of the mountain, or you'll find me on the side of that mountain dead with my hand reaching out to the other side." No matter what, that's what you have to look out for when you're associating with people. Do they have a high level of ambition or a high level of influence and integrity? All three go together — ambition, influence, and integrity. And all those three together, man, that's what creates that startled cat's speed.

You have got to want it so bad that you have a tear coming out of your eye when you're explaining your company, like I did when I was young.

I was fighting for love. And when you fight for something that's powerful, there's nothing that can stop you. To me, God is love. That means you have God with you as your business partner praying and saying, "Hey, you and me, we're business partners." So that's what keeps me going. No matter how tough it gets.

Just remember that we're all human beings. We're all here to go through and learn. It's so amazing to get a touchdown in the end-zone when there are 3 minutes left to go and you're down, and you have to fight to own the end-zone. Everybody's cheering. Then you get lifted up by the crowd, and you're saying, "Wow! Look, I did it! I did it! I did it! We did it! We did it as a team!" And you look at everybody's eyes, and they look in your eyes, and they know that we did it together.

It's like in the movie *Lord of the Rings* when he finally gets through the mountains. He gets carried up to the Mountain of Doom, and doesn't think he can make it another step. Sam carried him until he could get that one last bit of strength. When all is said and done and he wakes up after being saved by the eagles, he looks at all the people coming in. There was that moment when Frodo looked at Sam when he came in and they both just paused in the moment. They looked at each other's eyes, and they remembered all the challenges they had gone through together. They knew it right when they looked into each other's eyes.

That's a partnership, a real business partnership. It is amazing when you can look at your friend and say, "Wow — think of what we've been through together," without saying a word. You CAN develop a friendship group like that, like we have here. We can change the world. That's what it's all about.

## Daily time management

I have a mission now to create that movement with generation Y and I have an action plan for it. I've always been the type of person who calls my friends all the time and they'll call me. I spend time with them and really talk to them. That always leads to something. But I have the faith inside myself to know that God is leading me in the right direction, that faith is leading me in the right direction. And it always has.

I wake up with expectation every morning. I think really into the future, but don't forget about the past. I recognize it and move on. I focus on the present, focus on the future. And I'm always doing what I can to move myself forward to that future because that future is pulling, always pulling. Your destiny is pulling.

We are being pulled by our destinies, no matter what we do. As soon as we open up our eyes in the morning, our philosophy, our mindset, will lead us to where we're supposed to go. So trusting in that is very important.

Work so much on your faith, belief, and trust that, all of a sudden, they become almost automatic suggestions. All of a sudden, I am on the phone making a deal, writing an article for a magazine, or writing some type of proposal or vision outline, and I sit back and, well, it's done. I look at it and pat myself on the back. I realize that I got it done based on my drive, my desire.

Read *Think and Grow Rich*. That book has created many millionaires around the country and around the world. It talks about desire pretty much before anything else. Desire will drive you to do the actions you do everyday. So when you ask me what I do everyday, I do something different every day. Isn't that great?

In the movie *Groundhog Day,* Bill Murray wakes up every day to the same exact thing. In the end, it was love that finally freed him from that predicament. Imagine doing the same thing over and over and over again, just as you might in business, but as soon as you find that love or that passion, you are freed from the prison of complacent repetition.
I live my life free because no matter what happens, I have those friendships. I have the philosophy. I have the destiny, the vision. Nothing will stop me. I've got God on my side. I've got me on my side. I've got my friends on my side. If you have all that on your side, what can stop you? And if you know that in your heart, then it will come up to your mind. And your mind will direct you to take the actions that you need to take, which will create the results that you want. It all starts in your heart.

It's all about desire. What's your motivation? What's the "why" that makes you cry?

## Growing exponentially

How to expand your number of friends exponentially? How to increase your sphere of influence to explode so you can get a lot of people in the business (lead generation)? A great thing that I discovered when I'm networking in a big event is that I want to make sure that the event is compatible with me. If you're a basketball player and you go into a football event, you'll feel kind of left out. As soon as that basketball player goes into a basketball event, they feel great because they feel like everybody around them understands them. My good mentor, Robert Butwin, used to always tell me, "the key to the word relationship is the ability to relate."

I remember being in a big city once where we went to the Ritz Carlton for this event where we planned to see a team member. It turned out to be a business entrepreneurs event where we didn't know very many people. They were all businesspeople, but not in the world of network marketing. We all ended up leaving when I felt uncomfortable there.

In contrast, as soon as I got on the MLM cruise, or I'm in a network marketing event, my energy lights up. That flame inside me just gets bigger and grows because everybody understands one another and what we've all been through. I understand what you've been through. You'll let me know. But if someone's in a different business, they just don't get it.

When I'm prospecting or friend-making, as I like to call it, we can do as Dale Carnegie says in *How to Win Friends and Influence People:* smile, remember their name, shake their hand, and give them your attention. Pat them on the back and make them feel important and proud of themselves. I just think that is something that's natural. I love it.

When I'm in that room of network marketers, I give up on caring about decided to have fun together. As you take the pressure off and are having fun with someone, you build this friendship. And all of a sudden, something happens. You could next be working together making millions of dollars and helping a lot of people.

All in all, it comes down to who you end up sitting next to in the cab or end up walking into the elevator with. It's not about your business card or collecting business cards. It's about making friends. When I talk to someone, even if they are in the same business and I don't feel that immediate connection, I let them go. Sometimes I walk up to someone and feel like they're someone I've known forever, even though I've just met them. Has that ever happened to you? I look for those people. And if I find those people, it's just natural for me to hang out with them and build a relationship. That's professional network marketing or professional friend-making right there.

So if you're in an event, and you walk up to someone and they start telling you their life story, you're not getting along, you don't really care, or you're not really listening, it might not be a good fit. You know they always say, "Always listen more than you talk." Well, it's a lot easier to listen rather than talk if you actually go up to someone with whom you can relate.

Say you go up to someone you relate with and you really love snow boarding, and they start talking about snow boarding in the Swiss Alps. You think, "Oh really? That's cool!" And all of a sudden, you listen, because you like to listen. So put yourself around people that you can relate with more, and stop spending so much time with the people that you can't relate with because they'll find out. They'll find people with whom they can relate, and that will help them out more.

For example, if you're at an event where someone comes up to you and you don't feel connected, just politely shake their hands and say hello, listen politely for a moment, then excuse yourself. Then go find someone else with whom you relate well because only then are you going to build a true relationship. Dale Carnegie says, "Be genuinely interested in others." But make sure that you meet someone whom you're genuinely interested in because that will build a relationship. That will bring true friends. Great friends. That will build your culture, your community, your tribe. That sets where you're going.

This is all part of the movement. And all of us together can help change all these millions of young people's lives. We can maybe save a lot of lives. Because they can have something that makes them say, "Wow! I can do it!" "Someone believes in me!"

It's so amazing to see a young person, how much they can change, when someone, whether baby boomer or generation X, says, "I believe in you. Join this movement with me."

And you'd be surprised — that one statement could have saved them from committing suicide. That one statement: "I believe in you." I'm getting chills right now. That could save their life. And how amazing would that be when they're walking onstage telling their story of how they did it, and they say 'thank you' to you, because you helped them get there. That's what this movement's all about.

— Dakota Rea

# FROM ZERO TO MILLIONS STRATEGY

· Remember FBT: Faith, Belief, and Trust.
· Associate with like-minded people or communities.
· Be genuinely interested in others.
· The key to the word "relationship" is the ability to relate.
· Build relationships.
· Keep your friendships strong.
· Have integrity and be an example for others to follow.
· Enthusiasm on fire is better than knowledge on ice.
· Read *The Speed of Trust* by Steven M.R. Covey.
· Do friend-making, instead of prospecting.

# CHAPTER 3

# IF GREAT IS AN OPTION, HOW DARE YOU SETTLE FOR GOOD!

Lior, tell us a little bit about yourself and your journey towards Network Marketing rock star status?

I t's kind of humbling being here, first of all. Thank you for the opportunity to say a few words about myself.

I actually started about two and a half years ago and I was a traditional business owner. I had a consultant company and Microsoft was a client of mine, so I was working about 50, 60, 70 hours a week and I didn't want to work 50, 60, 70 hours a week.

What I learned growing up was Plan A and Plan B. Plan A is that you go to school, you graduate, you get a job, you work 40 hours a week for the next 40 years of your life, and then you retire and die; there's a great life. But I didn't like Plan A.

Plan B is you go to school, you graduate, you start your own business, you work 50, 60, 70 hours a week for the next 40 years of your life and then you retire and die; there's a great life. I didn't like Plan B either.

I actually remember one day I was sitting in Microsoft's head office in Toronto and looking out this nice big window at all the people enjoying the sunny day while I sat behind a desk and I just wondered to myself, "What am I doing here? I'm just wasting my life away." And then I remember looking into the office and there were about a hundred other people in the office also looking outside of the windows!

That's when I realized that we were all just wasting our lives. There has to be more to life than me spending 8 hours a day sitting in this office making the president millions of dollars a year. I felt like a slave. I felt like I was in a scam. I felt like somebody was tricking me. I felt like I was being used because I knew that my potential was much more than what I was currently given.

Sounds like a pyramid scheme! That's the real pyramid scheme because you have a president, you have a vice president, you have senior managers, managers, employees, and what does that look like? Looks like a pyramid, right? And all the money goes to the top.

Now in network marketing, even the people at the bottom can make as much money as the person at the top. So that's why it's not a scheme or a pyramid like traditional businesses are or like being an employee because you have the same potential as anybody else in your organization. And it all depends on a few things which we'll get into.

So when I started to realize this, I said, "Okay, I need a Plan C," and I started to educate myself. I knew that there was some knowledge and information that I was missing. And I saw people in the world outside my window who were living whatever lives they wanted to live, so I said, "How do I do that?"

That's when I started to find books like *Rich Dad, Poor Dad* by Robert Kiyosaki and Secrets of the *Millionaire Mind* by T. Harv Eker and started listening to Tony Robbins and developing myself. This was actually the first time I started to learn about the concept of passive residual income. You do the work once and you get paid for the rest of your life. I thought, "Hey — that would allow me to be that person on the other side of 'this window' and enjoy the day, right?" So I started to look into who is using this concept in the world.

I started to understand that authors write their books once and every time their book sells, they get paid over and over again. Musicians make their CD once and every time their CD sells, they get paid over and over again. Real estate investors buy properties, rent them out, and there's the monthly cash flow there, especially with the right kind of cash flow that you make. And I said, "Ok, now, what do I do?" So that's when I started to learn about something called network marketing, something that will allow you to do the work once, build an organization, and leverage the efforts of other people.

In 1957, Jay Paul Getty was the world's richest man, and he said, "I would rather make 1% of a hundred people's efforts than a 100% of my own." He was the world's richest man, so he obviously understood the power of leveraging the efforts of others, and I said, "That's what I need."

I started to do my research and found that there were thousands of companies out there that are doing this. Some are better than others in certain ways. There's leadership, there's compensation, there's support, sponsors, there are all these things that you have to look into when you're choosing the right opportunity.

I was approached by a friend of my ex-girlfriend at that time and she basically came to me and asked me to look at this opportunity. It turned out to be in designer props like watches, gold, diamonds, and jewelry, and they were basically competing with Gucci, Louis Vuitton, and Chanel. I wasn't really a designer person and had never even worn much jewelry, even a watch.

She asked, "How would you like to get paid to wear your watch?" And I said, "Well, that's interesting, but number one — I work 50, 60, 70 hours a week, and number two, me and jewelry — that's really not my thing." I actually said "no" to her for about six months.

And now I realize how much money that cost me, but she kept coming back to me with some checks that she was making in the business. I remember looking at these checks: $2000 a week, $3000 a week, $4000 a week. You know, I looked at her and I looked at these checks and I said, "So how many hours a week are you working?" She said, "A few." I said, "Okay, well now you're speaking my language. Let's take a look at what this is."

So I went down to the head office which was located in Toronto, Canada, which was the same city where I lived. I met the President and the CEO and I asked them questions for four hours because I really wanted to know what I was getting involved in from a business point of view. I realized that they were doing something that nobody else in the world was doing, they had no competitors for the type of products that they were marketing, and they were creating a million things. I said, "Okay, well, now I want to get on board." So I did my research. I did my due diligence and once I did have all the information that I needed, that's when I made my decision to get started.

When I got started, I had zero experience in network marketing. I mean, I've been doing sales since I was 16 years old and I've done tele-marketing for almost every product you could ever dream of. I've sold credit cards over the phone, I've sold mortgages over the phone, I've sold cell phones over the phone, and I've sold free estimates for windows and doors over the phone. By far, the easiest thing I've ever had to do from starting to work at the age of 16, was my first business experience: sales over the phone.

Then I progressed to what I thought was much better, which was walking around the city with luggage filled to the brim with a coffee machine. I went from business to business to business, trying to sell them this coffee machine. I did this in the middle of the summer, in a full suit, lugging around this heavy coffee machine, sweat pouring down my face, and wondering why these people wouldn't buy my coffee machine. Hmmm…that was pretty interesting.

My next business experience was with the IT world. I started working for this company called Soft Choice, which sells products that are IT-related. So I built up my experience from a business to business point of view having come from a business to consumer one. Eventually, I got hired by Microsoft. My goal with Microsoft was to show them that that they needed me to the point where I could quit and take them on as a client.

So that's what I did. I started working there, and they saw that I was a pretty good employee, so I quit and told them that if they wanted my services, they'd hire my company. And that's what they did. So then I had Microsoft as a client and that's how I progressed on to where I was when I had my epiphany.

When I started network marketing, I had all this great sales and business experience, had a degree in marketing and entrepreneurship from Wirestone University, one of the best business schools in Canada. Not only did I have an excellent marketing education, but I had also taken quite a few psychology courses because I was very interested in how the mind works.

So there I was with all of this experience and the first thing the networking company told me was "forget everything that you know." That's very hard for a sales person, mostly because as sales people, we have very big egos, but also because we all like to think we know more than everyone else.

I learned that the reason you must forget everything that you know is that in network marketing, it has nothing to do with what you know, and everything to do with learning a system and then duplicating that system over and over and over again. I thought, "It's that simple? Really? All I have to do is learn a 1-2-3-4 system which is what my company had and then I just have to do that over and over and over again? They said yes, but that didn't mean I was going to listen.

I tried it my own way for a little while, but that didn't work out. Through trial and error, I learned that I needed to listen to what they said. In the first month of being in this company, I actually generated very close to the same income that I was generating in my business. I thought, "Wow, this is great!"

At the time, I was still working 50, 60, 70 hours a week, so I could only do my network marketing 5 hours a week. But that first month showed me that this is working. It gave me the belief that maybe this is something that I could do.

I had heard so many other stories about people getting started and now working full time in their networking business. But I didn't have the belief just yet that this would work for me. But little by little, my trust and belief in what I was doing kept growing.

There are 3 things that you need to develop if you want your belief to go from "just belief to knowing." And there's a big difference between belief and knowing. For example, you know that you have a left hand; that's a fact. Nobody can tell you that you don't have a left hand. So I'm at that level now, where I know I can do it. When I started out, I believed I could do this business, but now I KNOW that I can do this business. There is a switch that has to take place, for somebody to go from belief to knowing, and it has to come in three different areas.

## Know and Believe in Your Company

The first area you have to have belief and knowing is in the company that you're working with. You have to understand the company, its heritage, its roots, and its products. You must know where the products come from, use the products, wear the products, understand what's unique about them, and understand what's special about them.

In addition to that, know the company as well; understand where your leadership has come from, understand their experience, understand they are willing to support you as a distributor. You have to really learn and educate yourself about the opportunity that you're in and go from just believing that this is a good opportunity to knowing 100% that you have the best company and the best products in the world, and nobody is going to tell you otherwise.

Do you see the little switch there? From I believe it, to I know. Just like it's a fact that I have a left hand, it's a fact that I am in the best company in the world and have the best products in the world. So that's number one.

## Know and Believe in Network Marketing

Number two, you have to have that same kind of belief in knowing the terms of the industry and in the terms of the profession of network marketing. You have to go from just believing that this is something that can give you a part-time income to knowing that this is going to give you the lifestyle that you want and is going to help you make a difference in people's lives.

Again, there's that difference and in order to educate yourself, you've got to meet people in this profession who are already building big down-lines and are creating six-figure, even seven-figure earnings. You have to go to events like the Mastermind event in Houston that I have attended. In this event, you're trained by people making at least a hundred thousand dollars a month. That raises your belief to knowing that this profession can give you something like that.

You have to read books, and you have to educate yourself. Once you believe in and know your company and its products and believe in and know the profession of network marketing, you've got two areas that have gone from belief to knowing.

## *Know and Believe in Yourself*

The third area that you need to go from belief to knowing is yourself. You start with your company and its products, move on to the profession, and then onto yourself. I call these three things "the pillars of success." If you're missing one of the pillars, what's going to happen?

Think of a tripod; it actually has three legs. If you take away even one of the legs, the whole camera falls down. Now, compare this analogy of the camera to your success and think of the three legs as companies and products, profession, and yourself. The stronger those three legs are, the stronger the foundation of your success will be.

In regard to yourself, you can't just believe that you can do anything: that's not enough. There's a different level that you can get to: knowing that you can do anything. This means knowing that regardless of the company you're with, regardless of the products you're showing people, regardless of what people say to you, you will be successful. There is no doubt in my mind that no matter what I do, I will be successful.

Now, I haven't always been this way. There were many times that I didn't believe I could be successful at anything. Unfortunately, there are many people in the world out there that are just like me. I want them to know that we all have the same potential. We can all do amazing, great, unbelievable things in the world. Just because you don't think that's you, doesn't mean it's not you. There could be some information or knowledge that you don't have yet that could raise you from belief to knowing that you can do anything in the world. The way you get to that knowledge is through studying personal development.

That's why I am who I am today. It's because of the books that I read, the videos I've watched, the seminars I've attended, the training I've received. Every time somebody speaks, I think about how this information can make a difference in my life. I do this every single time and that's because I know that whatever information I get from them is going help me.

You must go from belief to knowing the company and products, the profession, then yourself. Those are the three things that you have to develop.

In my journey, I started educating myself by reading books about the profession and talking to successful people. I sat down with the CEO and asked him questions for four hours, then with the VP because they had 60 years of experience. I knew that if they had all that experience, talking to them and learning all I could from them would help me.

Soon enough, I actually made about 3 or 4 times the money I was making with my own business. It was then that I knew it really did work. All of a sudden, my belief to knowing is going up and up because I proved it to myself. There's a difference between somebody telling you about it or seeing somebody do it and doing it for yourself. Your belief goes to knowing like THAT. If you want to raise your belief to knowing, experience is the fastest way to do it.

I believe the only reason I could get to that point was because I "washed my brain." People think brainwashing is such a negative word, but if somebody's going to brainwash you to be successful, let them brainwash you, right? Why not? Let them brainwash you so that you can have a great life. I "washed" my brain of everything I had learned since I was 16 years old, and I said, "I'm going to be coachable."

Now, each and every person has a different definition for what coach-able means. I'll tell you my definition of coachable. Being coachable means that even if you don't understand why somebody's telling you to do something, even if you don't agree with it, even if it doesn't make sense to you, even if you don't want to do it, do it anyway. Because, obviously, that person is telling you to do it because they've had some success doing it, so why not try it?

I decided to take on being coachable. I decided I was going to be a blank slate. Whatever you tell me to do, I'm going to do it. That's very hard for a lot of people, to give up control like that!

A lot of people think someone will try to make them do something negative. But you have to realize that if you just do what people in this profession are asking you to do, you're going to live a great life.

Everything that they tell you to do, unless it is wrong or outside the law, DO IT, because you'll never know what difference that will make for you. And if it doesn't work for you, at least you have tried it. Then you can try something else. But don't just disregard it because you think that it's not going to work for you. The only way you'll actually know if it's not going to work for you is if you do it and it doesn't work for you.

Going back to my story, here I was making really good money in my first 3 or 4 months when something happened. Some family came to me and said, "There's a great opportunity to go to Moscow, Russia, and do some real estate." I don't know why I agreed to do that, but I did.

So here I am in Moscow, Russia, again working 40, 50 hours a week for the rest of my life. The only difference was because of the first few months that I had started my network marketing business, I kept getting these bonus checks every single month. So that proved to me that what they told me was going to happen did happen. I did the work once and I got paid every single month; it was actually happening! This again made my belief and knowing go up.

It was at that point that working 50, 60 hours a week didn't make sense to me. I was working so hard, yet getting a check in the mail for doing nothing. Soon after, I quit what I was doing in Moscow and came back to Toronto.

That's when I really started to focus on that check that I was receiving every month, building it until it grew bigger and bigger and bigger. My goal and my vision had always been to uplift the lives of the people around me in my life. I thought about my mother.

My mother and I came to Canada when I was 5 years old and I saw how hard she was working. That's actually one of the things that motivated me to become a "hungry" individual. I wanted success more than anything else because I saw how hard she was working to give me a great life.

And I said, "First of all, I don't want to work that hard to have a great life." Because as hard as she was working, there was no way that I was going to get everything that I wanted in my life being an employee and working as hard as she was. And secondly, I wanted to give back to her for all of the things she did for me and to help my family and friends.

At the age of 20, I registered my first business. It was a promotional products company where you put the names of your company on the cupboard pens. That didn't work out, but at the age of 20 is when I actually decided there has to be more to life as well. There's always been that hunger inside of me. I wanted to help her and I wanted to help other people because I knew that my life could only become better if I made other people's lives better. When the lives of the people around me become better, my life will automatically become better. Automatically. And so I've been focused on that.

I started to imagine how I could one day show up at my mother's door with a check to pay off her mortgage or a check to pay off her car expenses or a check to send her on a trip around the world. I actually had this vision in my mind of taking all my family out for a nice dinner, then after dinner inviting them up one by one to ask what their dreams are and giving them the ability to go and live all of their dreams. I've had that vision and dreamt about it, imagining how happy they are actually being able to live their dreams.

So that's my driving hunger. While I've been focused on that, I've noticed that my lifestyle is increasing. I've upgraded from a Honda to a Mercedes SLR 500 convertible. It was really nice driving around in the summer. I bought a condo downtown by the lake and I have another condo a bit closer to our head office in Toronto.

I'm probably going to buy some more real estate in the near future because one of the things that I learned from Robert T. Kiyosaki's *Rich Dad, Poor Dad* is that I'm either working for my money or my money is working for me. And I'd rather have my money working for me. I'm using the money I make in this profession to invest in real estate that's going to keep my wealth continuing.

## Going on cruises and Jet Lag

I've been traveling recently to Israel, Russia, Europe, and the Caribbean, so it's been a pretty tough life. I don't know if people who don't know about this profession are ready for that kind of lifestyle. Right now we're on a cruise, I'm looking outside, the sun is setting, watching the waves, and we just came back from 3 different islands. We're eating too much and having too much fun. My experience over the past 2 1/2 years has been great. I'm already at that point today where I have the choice to not ever have to work again. Being 30 years old and having that choice and traveling around the world is amazing. I also feel good knowing that the family that I'm going to have one day — I'm not married, and I don't have children — will be able to have time that they need from their father.

I actually grew up for 20 years without a father. I met my father for the first time 10 years ago. I realized how important it is for children to have parents that can support them and that they can learn from as much as they can. I want to be there for my kids whenever they need me. If they want me to be their bus driver, I'll be their bus driver. Whatever it is that they need and want, now I know I'm going to have that. I would really like to have a large family.

## How to explode fast

Being coachable is very important. I brainwashed myself, scrubbed it clean, nice and squeaky clean. I made up my mind that whatever they told me to do, I would do it. I had no right to have an opinion because they knew what they were doing, and I didn't. I got rid of all of my excuses, all my opinions, every single thought that I had in my mind so that they could teach me.

Our CEO, his name is Carlos, has been in this industry for over 20 years. He's got 12-14 years of experience as a distributor and 6-8 years from the corporate side. This is a man who's made over 5 1/2 million dollars. I wondered how anyone could look at Carlos, who had become the top distributor in 4 different companies, and say, "No, I'm not going to listen to your 20 years of experience. It doesn't matter that you made 5 1/2 million dollars. It doesn't matter that you're telling me to do this. I'm just going to do what I want to do." That wouldn't make sense. He obviously has a system that he uses to become successful.

But a lot of people do that! They think they know better and that's fine. People are in different areas of their life. When I introduce somebody into my business, and they just start to do their own thing, I say, "OK, you go and do your own thing and when that doesn't work out, and you're ready for some results, then let me know, OK?"

This actually happened to our CEO Ramin, who was a very excited 19 year old when he got into this industry. His mentor told him the first thing he had to do was to make a list of 100 people, then call everyone on that list. All Ramin could think about was how quickly he could be successful in the business and how he could build it as quickly as possible.

His mentor responded that it would take about a year and a half. Ramin did not like that answer. He wanted to do it more quickly. And his mentor said that if he did not make a list, he would be back in 6 months wondering why he was not successful and why his business wasn't working. No matter what, after finally making that list, it usually takes about 6 months to one year before a business actually takes off and he'd never have to work again.

So, that's the reality of some people who get started; they think that there's some secret to building this business, but really, the foundation of successful people is very simple. You make a list, you pick up the phone, and then you call the people on the list with the person who introduced you to the company. You identify the person, tell the prospect a little bit about this person, all of their success, and then they have a conversation with each other. If interested, they come and see the opportunity. If it's not the right time, you follow up with them and keep building a relationship. If it is the right time for them, great! You get them going as quickly as possible, let them know how they can contact you, and let them know who their support team is.

In our company, we have something called the "line up support form" which has the top five people in the team that are already making 10, 20, 30, 40 thousand dollars a month that they can contact anytime they want with questions. If the first person is not available, they go to the second person, and so on.

When I first started, I had no idea what I was doing. I had no experience. I had nothing. All I had was this piece of paper with the names, phone numbers, and email addresses of people that could support me with anything that I needed at any time. If I didn't know how to do something, I would pick up the phone and say, "Hey Kristine, I want to call this person, but I don't really know what to say. Can you help me? Thanks." So we would all three go to the phone and she would have a conversation with that person. And if she wasn't available, I had four other people. So the support that I was receiving was just incredible; I have never seen anything like it in my life. What I liked about it was that anybody could get started with absolutely zero experience or knowledge, and they had all this support to help them get started. It was almost impossible for somebody not to be successful.

So, again, being coachable and using your support system is very, very important. You have to do the research on the person who's sponsoring you into the business. One of the tricks that I've learned when you're evaluating a sponsor is to ask that person for the contact information of 5 or 10 people in their down-line. Then call those people and find out how their up-line is and if they are getting the support they need. Ask if they are knowledgeable and are helping build their business?

It's almost like you're applying for a job; the employer is going to ask you for a list of references, because they're going to call and see if you're the right person to work for them. Well, now you're interviewing somebody who may be helping you so that you'll never have to work again. You want to work for somebody who is strong, powerful, and committed to you, somebody who's a leader, somebody who takes it seriously, somebody who's not going to joke around, somebody who cares about your success. These are the things that you want to look for.

Coachable, support, you want to make sure you have the right sponsor and you want to have the right attitude. You want to be positive. You want to do personal development training. I've done a lot of personal development training. I've conditioned my brain to block out as much negativity as possible. If it's something negative that can affect my thinking, I just get rid of it as quickly as possible, because that's not going to help me. And a lot of people are not very positive!

When I get started working with somebody, I put together a personal development plan. I tell them what I've done. I recommend the books, videos, movies, etc. that I've discovered that helped me. I encourage them to develop themselves to the point where nothing stops them, to the point where their brain is a well-oiled machine that can wake up in the morning and say, "I'm ready to create whatever I feel like doing."

We all have the power to create whatever life we want to create, but our brains are not programmed for that. The only thing that human beings ever want to do is to be comfortable. We are programmed to survive. That's it.

If you look at the world, there are millions and probably billions of people surviving, waiting to die. They are just surviving life, waiting to die. If you choose to, you're going to work all your life, and then you will die.

But what would you have really accomplished?

What kind of legacy would you have built?

Did you make this world a better place?

What will your children think of you?

Are you somebody who just worked until they died, or somebody who actually created the best life that they could?

You should strive to be somebody who loved life, somebody who wanted to make a difference. Can you imagine the difference in your children's lives when they can be proud of you for really making that kind of difference?

My father and mother had a job, and they worked really hard to support me, and I love them for that. But it's a much different kind of role model that you can be for your children, to say that you don't have to just survive and die. You can go out, you can do whatever you want, you can live whatever life you want, you can have passion, and you can love life. That's the kind of leader that you need to be for your team, for your people, for your company, for the world.

I'm doing this to create leaders that can change the world. I want to make this world something that people are proud of, not stricken with war, conflicts, and people who are waiting to die. I want to see everybody working together to create something bigger than we ever even imagined possible. I don't even know what that's going to look like and that doesn't even matter. All I know is that if I keep having that kind of thinking and keep developing myself, people will see me the way that I am right now, and they're going to want that. They're going to want to be inspired.

People want to be great. But, again, the brain is always going to come back to how do I survive? It's like every time I go and pick up the phone in the morning, I have to listen to the little voice in my head saying, "Uh-oh — you're picking up the phone and then you're going to call somebody, and they could reject you, or they're going to say it's a pyramid or whatever," and that little voice is going off in my head. What I say to that is thank you for sharing, but you are not going to give me a great life. Because the little voice in your head doesn't understand great life. It's not programmed that way! All it's programmed to do is to protect you. And if I put down the phone, I'm safe, I'm protected. I don't have to call anybody. I can just sit on my couch, watch TV, and survive until I die. And then the little voice in my head is saying, "You're safe, you're comfortable, you can survive now."

But that's not going to give me a great life, that's not going to inspire people, that's not going to have my family proud of me, that's not going to make a difference in other people's lives. That's just me surviving. I understand that, but many people don't understand.

They wonder why they aren't motivated and why they can't just get off the couch and do something. They don't understand why they can't wake up in the morning and just get on the phone and speak to people. Why are other people successful and they can't be like that?

Because they don't understand that's what it means to be human. What it means to be human is you will never want to deal with it, ever. It's not normal. It's not normal to get on the phone and call 20 people to figure out what they want to be, do, and have in their life; that's not normal. It's not normal to want to inspire thousands of people; that's not normal. It's not normal to do a presentation in front of 500 people, that's not normal. It's not normal to want to go out and just meet somebody on the street and talk to them; that's not normal.

When our CEO Ramin was starting in this industry, his mentor told him he was weird. "What do you mean, I'm weird?" he asked. His sponsor explained that he was weird because he was willing to do what 99% of the people in the world are not willing to do. He was part of the 1%. You have to be weird to do what we're doing. You have to be not normal. You have to really embrace being weird. Being "not normal" and weird means you're doing something that's going to make you successful.

Someone once said that "progress belongs to the unreasonable man." And if you're reasonable, you'll only do things that have been done before. And then there's no progress!

What's more, the results of reasonable people are not impressive, they're just reasonable. You have to be weird and abnormal to create unreasonable results. That's one thing that I said to myself. I'm willing to be weird. I'm willing to be abnormal. I'm willing to have people laugh at me. I'm willing to have people not agree with what I'm doing. I'm willing to have people say that I'm part of a pyramid. I'm willing to have people not agree with anything that I'm doing. Because I know that if I do that, 99% of the world is not doing it. So I'm always doing what nobody else is doing.

When I was at the Mastermind event in Houston, for example, I was the only one from my company there. So while I'm sitting there, I'm thinking to myself, hey I'm doing something that nobody else in my company is doing. Now I'm being successful. Now I'm doing what it takes to be a leader. Because that's what leaders do. They do what 1% of the people in the world do, not what the other 99% of the people are doing.

Now I'm on this cruise right now and the only one from my company here and I'm very proud of that. I'm telling myself, "I'm a leader. I'm setting an example for other people." This is what you have to do in order to really stand out, in order to really have a huge success in the world: to do what nobody is willing to do. By doing that, I know that I'm inspiring people all over my company.

I've been checking my Facebook page, posting pictures of my trip on Facebook, and posting my experiences of meeting all these people. One of my status updates was: I just woke up at 10 o'clock this morning, had a nice buffet breakfast, had a massage, went for a swim, went for a tan, played some cards, then I said, "Does your Monday look like this?" Then I put some pictures taken of the beach, people swimming, and the lifestyle.

Almost as soon as I posted, I got all these responses, one of them being from someone on my team who said, "Lior, I just quit my job." He added, "When you come back to Toronto, we're sitting down and going to take this all over the world."

This is how you need to lead people, by example. People are not going to do what you say. They will do what you do. You just show people what you're doing and the results you're getting in your life. Show them the lifestyle that you are living because you are willing to do what nobody else is willing to do.

Going back to your question, what did I do in my first month to generate all those results? I had the right thinking, I was willing to be weird, I was willing to be coachable, I was willing to listen, and I applied what I was doing. Every time that little voice in my head told me that I was about to die, I just ignored it because it didn't know what I'm doing or where I was; it just knew that the reactions in my body were uncomfortable.

So, every time I heard that, I said, "Thank you for sharing. You're not going to help me have a great life and I'm going to do what I've been told to do and I'm going to follow the system," and that's what I did. That's why I experienced the results that I was able to experience. And I was hungry for success. Nothing was going to stop me. You don't want to do business, great. Let's be friends and on to the next prospect. Remember: SW, SW, SW, SW, or some will, some won't, so what, someone's waiting. Someone's waiting for this opportunity.

I look at it like this: I'm walking through a forest and I'm just looking for the purple trees, but there are all these brown trees. So I see brown tree, brown tree, brown tree, purple tree. Great! OK, this is the person I've been looking for. So, really this isn't a sales business. It's a sorting business. I'm just sorting through people until I find the people that are ready. Now, it doesn't mean that brown trees are bad, or they're not good people, or even that I'm never going to want to work with them. It just means that they're not ready right now.

I say this profession is for everybody, but not everybody is ready for this profession. One day they will be ready. One day they're going to realize working 40 hours a week is not what they want to do. One day they're going to realize that spending more time with their kids is what they actually wanted. One day they're going to realize that they're spending too much on their taxes. One day they're going to realize that they want to travel more and their jobs will not let them do that.

It's just that right now, they're comfortable and they're okay with their life, so they're not ready. But there are all these purple trees out there that are so hungry and so ready and that's what inspires me every day — knowing they're out there. And I know the only thing that's in the way of me meeting them is me meeting them.

How do I find those purple trees? In my first month, when I got started, remember that I listened to exactly what they said to me. What did they say? They said to make a list of at least a hundred to 250 names, encircle the top 7, who I either had the trust in or the biggest relationship with, and call those people first. I did that. And actually while I was sitting there, and I was looking at the opportunity for the first time, I actually said to myself what a lot of people say to themselves: who do I know that will be interested? I went through and thought, "No, she won't be interested, he won't be interested," and so on.

I was actually speaking on the phone with one of those people who I thought wouldn't be interested in the business, and I said "You know, I'm just going to mention it to you." I didn't have any knowledge because this was my second day, but I was excited. I had the enthusiasm. Our CEO Ramin always says, "Light yourself on fire with enthusiasm, and people will come from miles to see you burn."

So I was on fire with enthusiasm, and people are attracted to that. So I got on the phone and said, "You know, Kim, I just got started with something and this opportunity is amazing. It's going to help me to never have to work another day in my life. I know that with what you're doing you need some extra income. You don't want to do that for the rest of your life, so you have to come and take a look at this. Don't ask me any questions. You have to come and take a look at this."

And the only reason that I could have said that to him is because we had that like and trust already. We had that relationship. There's no way I could have walked out to somebody in the middle of the street and said that to them, because they would have been like, "Who are you?" But he knew me well enough to say, "Ok, I'll come and take a look at that."

So he said he would come, and that was the first shocking thing, that he actually said, "Sure, I'll take a look at it." That first night that he saw the opportunity, he joined. Then he went home, went to sleep, woke up in the morning, told his wife about it, and his wife said, "What did you do?" Then she came and took a look at it, loved it, and joined as well. Then she went home, told her brother about it — he was a pilot — and her brother came and joined in as well. Next, he went home and told his parents about it; his parents came and they joined as well. Now, remember, this is the same person whom I thought would not be interested in the business.

I had discounted him. After that experience, I don't prejudge anybody. I tell every single person. That doesn't mean that they're ready for it, or that they're going to be the leader I'm looking for, but who am I to take away something that's going to make such a big difference in somebody's life? And how do I know why they're going to be interested in it — for the taxes, for the traveling, for the lifestyle, for the family, etc.?

Now I tell everybody to make their list, call the top 7 hotshots that you have the biggest like and trust with. That was something that I did right away and that's what had me have that huge success in my first month. Another thing that I did was start to work with the people that I introduced into the business.

For example, there was this new guy that just joined that was making his list of a hundred people and his top 7. So we'd sit down together and look at his list of 7 and call those people together. Then, one of those people would join, one of those being his brother, George. So then we got on the phone, made a list with his brother's people and started calling his brother's list. Then after his brother found somebody that wanted to do the business, we had that person make a list and call that person's list.

All of a sudden, my friend's team just starts growing and growing and growing, and obviously my team also starts growing and growing, because he's in my team. So, now I'm helping him, I'm helping his people's people, and so on, and this is growing and growing and growing. That's what I did in my first month.

I just helped my people with their people, and their people's people, and so on, and now everybody's happy because everybody's earning. That's what I have been duplicating. I find one person who's really hungry, tap into their list, and then help the person with their list. If you just do that, you don't need anything else, because every person has a list.

Think of all the people you would invite to your wedding, how big is that list? Now think of all the people in your Facebook, how big is that list? Think of all the people in your phone, how big is that list? Think of all the people whom you meet every day. I talk to people at the gas station, I talk to people in the mall, I talk to people at the convenience store, I talk to my dry cleaner, I talk to every single person I meet. I have a journal and in this journal, I have my list. I put everybody on my list, and then I follow up with these people. And when I meet them, I'm not talking to them about the business, I'm just talking to them about themselves, something that we train people in our business to do, and it is called like and trust.

Like is about them, trust is about you. So, if you want somebody to like you, what do you have to do? You have to get them talking about themselves. Because, for some reason, when we start talking about ourselves, we think we like the person because now we're talking about ourselves, right? And that person cares about us because they're asking questions about us. As soon as I meet somebody new, when I walk away from that person, I know where they live, if they're single, married or divorced, how many kids they have, what they like to do, if they like to travel, and I know what excites them. In 5 or 10 minutes, I know more about that person than maybe even someone they've known for years. Because I've taken the time to really be interested and care about them.

"People don't care about how much you know until they know how much you care."

And I've spent that time to show them — "Listen, I really care about who you are as a person and what you want." So I spend that time and because I've spent that time, now they like me. So like is there. Trust comes in when they know that I can help give them what they want and that I'm doing whatever I'm doing for the right reasons. That's when I share with them my story and share with them other people's stories and testimonials of success.

If I'm speaking to somebody and they say, "You know, I have a family, and I work 40, 50, 60, 70 hours a week and I really want to spend more time with them." Then I say, "You know, you should meet one of my business partners, Jamie Maldwin, whose wife's name is Monica. Monica actually used to be an IBM programmer and he used to be an IT manager for a tax consultant company. They got started in the business and all they ever wanted to do was to have kids and spend more time with them. In six months, she was able to quit her job at IBM and in a year and a half, he quit his job at the tax consulting company. About a year ago, they had a beautiful baby boy named Alex. They've been able to spend the whole year raising him, and they make about $25-30,000 a month."

And at this point, this person is probably wiping the drool from their face, and if you've done it the right way, they're probably looking at you thinking, "Ok, what do you do and how can I do that?"

You've just created all that curiosity, all that interest. Why? Because you took the time to understand what they want and you connected it with somebody who's already having that success. As soon as you do that, you've now bridged what they want with "I have what they want."

So, the bridge is the testimonial. The bridge is my story. The bridge is a real-life example of somebody who's experiencing what they want. When I put in that bridge, now they have what they want and the viewpoint that's going to get them there. It's not even a thought. Of course they're going to ask me what I do!

## Create curiosity

Then they ask me, "What do you do?" Now the tables are turned and they're coming after me. Some people might say that's sneaky or you're trying to trick people. Of course I'm trying to trick people; I want them to have what they want in their life. Because if they keep thinking the way they're thinking, they're not going to have what they want. I'm trying to trick them into having a great life.

They're not programmed to think that way yet. But when I get them, I'm going to work with them and I'm going to make sure they're on personal development. I will make sure they understand everything and that the only thing that they're going to have is the life that they want to have. But they're not ready for that yet, because life teaches you that you can't have everything you want. But I teach people that they can. And then I give them the tools and the systems to have what they want. That's all I'm focused on — other people.

I know if I help as many people as I can get what they want, I will automatically get what I want. It's not even a question. So, I just focus on how I can help people as much as I can. You want to build a relationship and get as interested in that person as you possibly can. And if they're not ready, fine, let's be friends, let's stay in touch. Whenever they're ready, they'll come to my Facebook page, they'll see all the things that I'm doing, and they'll get inspired themselves. They're seeing me living this great life, and they're going to be like you, asking themselves "What am I doing? What am I wasting my time for?" There are so many people who, for the past 2 or 3 years, I have told them about my opportunity, but 2 or 3 years ago, they weren't ready. Now, they see my cars and my condos, my lifestyle, and my cruises, etc. and they are like, "Tell me again what you do; let's talk again."

Because I'm living a really great life over here, they are interested. And if they want that, we'll have a conversation. I find out what they want.

Then I want to show them what they need to do in order to have that monthly income that they want to have.

It's so simple, you know. But people's brains, they just make it so complicated. And that's why I do this: to meet people who are like me, who have the hunger, and who are willing to sit down and say, "What's possible? What's possible for my life and how can I have it? "

That's my favorite thing in the world. Nothing, nothing is better for me than taking somebody who wants something and doesn't know how to get it, helping them get it, and then watching how happy they become when they have their way. Nothing is better.

## Habits to grow on

They say that 90% of what we do is habitual. One of the habits that I've developed is personal development every single day. I do 15 to 30 minutes in the morning, 15 to 30 minutes before I go to bed, and if I'm in my car and I'm not talking to somebody on the phone, I listen to a personal development CD. I'm programming myself.

It's kind of like when people go to the gym in the morning, when they leave the gym, they always feel better because the endorphins are going. I hate the gym, by the way, but I always feel great when I leave. It's the same with personal development. After I'm done, my brain is ready to go for the day.

When I listen to 15 to 30 minutes of personal development in the morning every day, my brain is ready to make calls, to meet people, to help make people's lives better. I'm ready for that. I'm inspired. Then I look at my vision board. My vision board is what my life is going to look like in 2-5 years. It's funny, because I had a vision board, and on my vision board, I had the car that I have today, the condo I have today, and the places that I wanted to travel. So, after today, I said, "I have to create a new vision board!" You should be creating new vision boards all the time.

And so I look at my vision board in my home office, which is actually on the doors of my closet. I have pictures and sayings and while I'm working, if I get some negative thought, or I get uninspired, I just look up. I see everything that I want to have in the next 2-5 years, and I'm right back down and going at it. You can't allow your brain to control your motivation.

You have to have external sources. On my laptop, I have a little saying everyday. I create who I am going to be that day. I create that. I don't let life tell me who I'm going to be. I create who I'm going to be that day. So I'm going to be energetic, passionate, and motivated, because my being affects my doing, which affects my results.

Some people think your "doing" affects your results, then results affect your being. What you do is what you have, and then you view what you have. But you have to start with yourself first. Who are you going to be today, so that you can do whatever you want to do and you can have what you want to have. It always has to start with you.

It's be-do-have! I create who I want to be. I look at my vision board. In my car, I have little sayings. On my rear mirror, I have something that I read. I always have an external trigger for my brain to be motivated. Because I know that if I don't do that, my brain will just want to sit on the couch and watch TV.

The typical person has all negative things distracting them. The TV is on, radio is on, and it's all negative, negative. CNN is "constantly negative news." Unfortunately, there is no news channel that gives you positive news all day. So you can turn on the TV and it's okay that you watch the TV. Because now that inspires you everyday, right. So that's what I'd do, then I'd plan my day.

When I do plan my day, what I put into my calendar is not "Call Tom at 6 pm." If I look at that, is that inspiring? No. So what I do is actually change that to "Call Tom at 6 pm and have a conversation with him about what it's going to take for him to be able to have the life that he wants to live." Or if I already know what Tom wants, I would put "how do I help Tom travel around the world and really experience things he has never experienced before?" So now when I look at that, I am excited to call Tom and get into that conversation. Always write something that inspires you.

If I'm going to have lunch, for example, I would not just put "Lunch at 12." I'm going to put "nourish my body with energy and fuel to allow me to have the energy to make as big a difference as I can." I always put something that's going to inspire me and get me into action.

So I start my day with personal development and make sure my calendar inspires me, and then I make calls. We have something in our organization called the "forensic network curve training system." This is a system that our CEO Ramin has created after making 5 and a half million dollars from four different companies over the past 20 years. This system tells me exactly what I need to do every single day in order to have the income that I want to have in order to have the lifestyle that I want. So I just follow the system.

Again, forget about what I know, and forget about what I've learned over my life. I look at the system and see what the system tells me to do. It tells me to make calls, to track it like this, to put it into this box, to check mark this when I'm done, so here's my stack of business cards that I may have gotten at a networking event.

Speaking of which, I go to lots of networking events, trade shows, and I meet many people on the streets. So I have this stack of business cards. I have my list of people that I want to call and Facebook contacts, so I get on the phone and call people. I always use a script as well; you have to have a script. So I use a script, get on the phone, and I don't even have to think.

You don't even have to think to make hundreds of thousands or millions of dollars. Pick up the phone, read the script, and based on what he says, I'll give him my answer. If it works out, that's great. If it doesn't work, I move on to the next person, then the next person, and the next person, and so on.

Eventually, I'll get to the point where I can actually leave the business and can go and live the rest of my life. According to this forensic networking training system, there's actually a point in time where you can stop doing your business and go and live your life. There's actually a point where you can do that.

And you know we have a binary system, so we have two lines. What it tells us is that once you have 2 to 3 people in each of your 2 teams who are making a minimum of 5 figures a month, so over 10 thousand dollars a month, you have people that are supporting your people. And that's what you want to have. You have people who will take care of your team and who are taking care of your people when you're not there.

Once you have that, you can safely go away and know that these people are taking care of your team. They're also creating people who are making 5 figures a month, so you're going to have much more than 2 or 3, but you need at least 2 or 3 who are really going out there and building the business. Then you can go and do whatever you want.

We've had people do that in two years. We've had people do that very, very quickly because of the compensation plan, our products, and our leadership. Because of all the different things that we do, I imagine in the next 2 years that I can safely leave this business. It's going to be difficult for me to not be doing anything, because I love helping people so much.

I'll probably be involved in this company for the rest of my life, but not as much as I am now, maybe 3 hours a week. But I'll still do 3-way calls, tell people my story, help people and teach them, and do seminars and trainings. But not too much, because I want to spend the time with my family and live the life that I want. More than anything, I want to help people be successful.

When I'm a hundred years old, ready to die and looking back at my life, I want to be able to say "I have no regrets." Zero regrets. Every single day, I ask myself, "What do I have to do today so that when I'm a hundred, I can look back at my life and say that I have no regrets?" And that's what I do every single day. So my routine is to get inspired in the morning, get on the phone, use my forensic network system, do my calls, help people, train people, and do the tours.

There are only 2 things that are helping you build your business. If you're doing anything other than these two things, you're not building your business no matter what you do. Number one is you're talking to people and having them come and see your opportunity. Number two is you're actually doing the presentation or the tour. If you're not doing those two things, no matter what you say, you're not building the business.

Those two things are going to allow you to build the business and everything else is secondary. You should either be talking to your people or showing somebody your business. That's what I do everyday. Because of our system, I don't need to guess how much money I am going to make this month or next month or how many calls I need to do. I know that if I want to make this much money this month, that I need to make so many calls. And if I make this many calls, out of all those calls, this many people are not going to be home, this many people are going to say no, this many people are going to say yes.

If I want to increase the amount of people that say yes, I have to make more calls. It's that simple. It's a numbers game and our CEO actually calculated, after speaking to thousands of people, that for every "no" you make around 16 dollars. So if somebody says "no," just say, "Thank you, you just made me 16 dollars."

When you have the kind of a mindset that no's are necessary for you to build this business, there is nothing negative. Everything is positive. And I just need to know that if I want to make this much money, I make this many calls. It's so simple.

## Mastermind groups

My mastermind group consists of my up-lines, the people in my business who are having the results that I want. I get together with them and we strategize, we brainstorm; they tell me what they're working on and what's working for them and I just work with them. I'm actually thinking about starting my own networking mastermind group in Toronto, Canada, for people from all different companies in different cities to come together to learn from each other's best practices, to learn how we can help each other become better at what we do.

This is a profession; it's not some MLM hobby that you're doing. It's a profession. And if you want to become better at your profession, you have to keep learning, educating yourself, attending events, speaking to people. So I want to get all these leaders together and talk. If we can build a friendship and inspire each other, that's great. My goal is to really improve and educate myself so that I can be the best leader that I can be. I can't control everything else, but I can control myself. So, I'll just focus on me and other people will see that and be inspired to do that too.

## Mentors

My mentors are the people in my business who are already successful and, of course, Ramin, my CEO. He has done it. He has a system. It works, step by step. And I just listen to what he says. If I have any questions, his door is always open. He's always available. His story is very interesting.

He actually got started in this industry when he was 19 years old. He was working at his parents' pizza store, flipping pizzas in the air all day. Somebody came up to him and asked if he liked doing this all day. He said he hated it. So the guy slapped a flyer down on the counter.

The flyer had a huge house and 10 cars with a guy standing there and it said, "Ask me how a man can make 70 thousand dollars a month selling cookies." He thought that must have been a typo; shouldn't that say cocaine or something? Because he didn't understand how you could make that kind of money selling cookies. He decided right then and there that he wanted to meet that man.

So they got into the guy's car and drove four hours to this guy's house. From Ottawa to Mississauga and he gets out of the car he sees this huge mansion and 10 cars just like in the flyer. He went inside and for five or six hours they talked. All this person was doing with Ramin was building a relationship, building rapport. Finally, at 3 o'clock in the morning, Ramin asked, "Well, how do I get started?" The guy responded, "You need about $2,300."

Ramin said, "I'm 19 years old, where am I going to get $2,300?"

So the man pointed to the window, and he said, "Do you see my 10 cars?" Ramin said that he did. "Which one is your favorite?"

Ramin said, "The Porsche; I love the Porsche."

The man said, "Ok, what if I told you that I really needed cash right now and I was going to sell you that Porsche for $2,300? You're telling me that in two hours you wouldn't be able to find the money to buy that Porsche for $2,300?"

Ramin said, "Of course, I would be able to find the money to buy that Porsche for $2,300."

So he says, "Whoever you were going to call to find the money to buy that Porsche, I want you to call them to find the money to get started in this business because what I'm promising you is a Porsche every single month for the rest of your life."

So, Ramin got on the phone at 4 o'clock in the morning, called one of his friends, got his credit card, and begged him to buy. He got started in the business and, in five years, made his first million dollars. Unfortunately, there were companies that went out of business and companies that changed their compensation plans, so he couldn't make as much money. So, he made a total of over 5 million dollars in four different companies and finally when the last company was supposed to ship him a big check, they went out of business, so he said, "That's it."

He couldn't trust anybody in the business. He could only trust himself. One time he woke up in the middle of the night and thought, "Wait a minute, I know how to do Network Marketing. I've proven that I can do it. And I have a connection with my family where I could create products and a system that nobody else can do. Only I have this connection with my family."

And so he created something so that all these casualties that were being left on the side of the road by all the defunct companies could come to his company. They knew that he wouldn't do the same to them because he had been deceived and treated badly too. His door is always open and he talks to people. He'll talk to somebody who has never had experience in network marketing.

He didn't need to do this. He had already made 5 million dollars, and he could have gone to an island and lived there for the rest of his life. But his vision was to create a thousand millionaires, because he thinks there are too many companies in this world that only make one or two people millionaires. Nobody else is making money. He doesn't understand that. Why give one person 15 million dollars when you can give 15 people one million dollars? If you're trying to help people, give as many people as you can a million dollars. That's going to transform this planet faster than anything else.

He's already created 11 millionaires. And I'm very proud that I'm going to be one of those. I'm also very proud that I'm going to be creating many hundreds of those millionaires as well. He's my mentor, because I know that whatever happens to the company or the industry, he's always going to look out for what's best for his people. I've seen him do it over and over again. I've seen him give up what he wants for what his people want, even if it doesn't really make sense for him.

When you meet this guy, you'll really start to see how passionate he is about helping people and how passionate he is about helping change the whole profession. He is somebody that I look up to. For somebody who had no experience at all to, in two and a half years, get to the point where I now know that I'll never have to work again, that's just because he has removed all the obstacles and barriers for people to make money. That's the only reason why I could do that. And we need more companies like that, and more people like that, and he's going to be the example of what it means to be a leader in this profession.

## Don't settle for good

About one month ago at my mastermind group, a passionate and inspiring individual in this business said, "If great is an option, how dare you settle for good?"

People deserve to have great lives. Every single person on this planet deserves to live an unbelievable life that they love. My focus is this: how can I help this person realize that they can go from belief to knowing that they can do anything and that the opportunity will give them a great life.

— Lior Skaler

## FROM ZERO TO MILLIONS STRATEGY

· Share your opportunity with everyone.
· Do the presentation or the tour every day.
· Have external triggers for your brain to keep you motivated, such as quotes, sayings, and vision boards.
· Study personal development materials 15-30 minutes a day, such as books, CD's etc.
· Be coachable.
· Sort out the right people for your business and stop selling.
· Create relationships.
· "Brainwash" yourself to follow the blue-print.
· Think of your business as a tripod: one leg YOU, second leg the products, and third leg the company.
· For each "no" that you hear when calling, you make $16.

# CHAPTER 4

# PICTURES ON MY WALL

Hi, Shannon, tell a little bit about who you are and your story about network marketing.

---

Okay. I was born in 1979. I'm 31 years old, married, and have two daughters, ages 3 and 6. I have worked from home for 15 years and the past 12 of those years I have been job-free. I live in a small town of about 8,000 people 30 minutes east of Lexington, Kentucky.

My first encounter with network marketing was through my dad's involvement. Dad was a network marketer amongst many other things. On any given day, he was juggling multiple businesses.

I was born into a farming family. We lived on a farm where we milked cows, raised Paso Fino horses, and grew tobacco. Growing up, we owned several "traditional" businesses, including a construction company, a heating and air-conditioning company, a geothermal well drilling company, an insulation business, a Mexican food restaurant and a mobile food concession van.

My dad developed a residential subdivision where he struggled to sell lots. I remember the stress that put him under and the fun things it kept us from, like family vacations and ball games. Dad was always working and we never had time or money to do the things we wanted to do when we wanted to do them. When we did take a vacation, it was usually in the car, a few hours up the interstate to a state park or to the nearby lake for camping. It was always somewhere cheap and usually only for the weekend. We couldn't stay long — we had work waiting on us back at home.

After the residential development didn't pan out, he decided to try a commercial development. He developed a strip mall shopping center where we opened our town's first Mexican food restaurant business. One of my sisters named it TYCles (the "TYC" stood for "Tacos, Yogurt, and Chili"), and I, along with my Mom and two sisters, were the employees. I'm not sure how much this business cost my dad to start, but it had to be a lot of money because of the equipment and other overhead. I think we topped out at around $200 a day in gross revenue, not enough to keep the doors open and the yogurt machines running. We would have sales of about $150 a day on average.

That is when we had the idea to take the restaurant on the road. We converted an old insulation van from one of my dad's other businesses into a mobile food concession van that we drove to festivals. That venture actually did better than the storefront! I remember us making thousands of dollars a day at some of the larger festivals. It was the inspiration for one of my childhood businesses.

I offered five paintball shots for $1 and grossed about $3,500 over the weekend at my first festival! I took the show on the road and set up my booth at other festivals like we did with our food concession van. Some festivals I would make money, others I lost money. The journey was fun and I got to spend a lot of time with my best friend and his little brother who helped me run it. We used to transport everything in a beat-up

1984 Plymouth Voyager van, the same van I drove my senior year of high school. You could hear it coming from miles away. It was a 4-speed stick-in-the-floor. Groovy, I know.

I noticed as a child that my dad was always very happy about one of his businesses in particular, his network marketing business. I remember when I was a little kid and was in the back of the room while he was up front giving presentations and drawing on a white board. I have very fond memories of that. I recall people clapping their hands and the excitement that he instilled in them. You could FEEL the energy in the room; it was good, positive energy that could take the darkest day and turn it into the most beautiful sun-filled day at the beach.

Dad passed away in 1996. It was my senior year of high school; I graduated in 1997. He was killed tragically in one of our businesses, the construction business. It was very horrific and unexpected, obviously, and that is the event that caused me to make a decision. Do I want to work for someone else? Or, do I want to go out on my own and create something for myself? At the time, I was a bag boy at a local Winn-Dixie grocery store. Dad's death really put a lot of things into perspective for me. I grew up really fast when he passed away.

I think a lot of networkers, especially those who are on this cruise with us, can recall a point in their past when they were caused to think about their future and make a decision. A lot of times that happens around a death, take my father's death as an example.

At that point in my life, I decided that I wanted to be a business owner. I wanted to make money for myself on demand from my mountaintop chalet while on a ski trip or from my beachfront home while relaxing with my family. I wanted to have a lifestyle where I could do whatever I wanted to do whenever I wanted to do it and I wanted to make money while doing it. I wanted freedom.

I remember reflecting back on the times that he and I spent together, which were few, really few, because he was always working; he was busy. I would think to myself, "I want to have money AND time. I want to own income-producing assets like real estate and other investments that produce a passive residual income way larger than my living expenses."

After my dad's death, I went on to college and, while I was in college, I got involved in network marketing. A friend of the family called me one night by mistake, thinking he was calling my mom. He had recently joined a company that had a weight loss supplement and he knew that my mom was a little bit overweight. He wanted to share the product with her, but he got me instead. I was 18 years old and skinny and didn't think I was really a candidate for the product, but he shared the opportunity with me instead. He said, "We're having a meeting and we would like you to come and see if you see an opportunity for yourself."

I went to the meeting and I remember it well. The presenter was using an overhead projector, the one with slides where you can write on them with an erasable marker. This was, I guess, before the video projector was prevalent. One of the slides was a geometric progression of numbers. It showed how you start with 5 people, and those 5 each finds 5, and then you have 25, 125, 625, and it just keeps multiplying. When you put dollar amounts beside those numbers, the dollar amounts also grow exponentially! They progress rather quickly, and you get up to where you realistically see $10,000 as a potential monthly income for yourself. It was intriguing.

I could not even imagine making $10,000 a month; WOW that´s a lot of money. I was making maybe $200 a week at the time, not quite even $1,000 a month, when I saw that slide for the first time. To see a $10,000 per month income potential seemed unbelievable, but I believed the numbers because I've always been really good in math and know that numbers don't lie.

I saw something for myself and immediately, when I saw that slide, I was sold. I mean, it doesn't matter what we're selling; we could sell rocks for that matter as long as people wanted them! I'm in! I can find 5 people that will see it like I see it and that was all that I had to do to start in network marketing.

At that point, I had a vehicle. It was a blueprint I could follow, and I had several people who were older than me, with far more credibility than me, and who knew more about it than me, who eagerly wanted to help me get it going. How could it get any better?

I had already met several people from the company that were making money, and I decided to join that company the night of the meeting! I made a few thousand dollars a month through retailing the products. I didn't really have any success at all in recruiting. I was 18 years old, very green obviously, and it is hard to get respect from your peers at age 18, especially those who don't know you — or so I thought at the time.

If something didn't go my way back then, I would make an excuse for it instead of owning up to it. I blamed my lack of success on outside variables when the problem was me. It wasn't my age; it was my confidence. By placing blame on my age, something I had no control over, the problem did not get resolved. Had I blamed myself and accepted it, I would have persisted until I had fixed the problem.

I was able to get a foothold in the industry through retailing products. That was good enough for me at the time. I was making more money from my part-time network marketing business than I had at any of my previous full-time jobs! I made enough money to avoid a job and put myself through college. I was a happy camper! From there, that led me to some other companies. I've been involved with about 12 companies, and I've had success with about half of them. I did very well with a couple of them and extremely well with one.

I was one of the top 10 distributors out of about 60,000 distributors in that one company. The company owner flew me and nine other people down to the corporate office to spend a week. They had arranged for a limousine that came and picked us up at the airport when we arrived. They flew us first class. It was my first time riding in first class. They put us up in a suite at a really fancy hotel right beside the beach. Everything, all the amenities one could imagine, they provided. They even asked us what we wanted to drink and the drinks were provided in the limo.

The next morning, the limo came and picked us up from our suites and took us to the corporate office. We got to the corporate office and, out in the parking lot, I saw several high-end sports cars. I saw a Ferrari — a red Ferrari with tan leather and chrome wheels, a black Porsche, and some other exotic vehicles. These were the owner's toys! When we walked into the boardroom, he had all of the keys laid down on the long table and he asked us, "Who wants to drive what this week?" Ever since I was a little boy, I have loved red Ferraris. I wanted to drive THAT one! I had a lot of fun while driving that car. It triggers emotions and an experience that you just don't get driving any other type of automobile.

So, I was driving down the road along the coast in a red Ferrari with tan leather and chrome wheels, a Modena 360, and I pulled up to get gas. About 8 or 10 people followed me in there and got out of their cars, surrounded my car, and started taking pictures. I felt like a celebrity. I felt very important when that happened and that, "Hey, this is where it all starts."

This event was like center stage for a lot of things. Two years later, I bought my dream car: a brand new yellow Corvette convertible with black leather seats, chrome wheels, a Borla exhaust system, and a Bose sound system. I bought a couple of vehicles, brand new, that I wrote checks for and didn't have to borrow against or use somebody else's money to buy them.

That was really nice and, for once, I felt that I was worthy. I did deserve this, I am a hard worker, and if I do a little bit more of this, then there are no limits. This is an infinite income business. The gears really started turning.

The company I had that really good run with went out of business eventually. From there, I went and did a couple of other things. I failed miserably at both of them. I made a few hundred dollars, maybe a few thousand dollars, but nothing life-changing. It was kind of a setback.

One of the companies I created that I have done very well with, and continue to do very well with today, is an email autoresponder service (http://www.contactbuddy.com). This company offers email autoresponder services to businesses.

Have you ever visited a website and signed up for their email newsletter? Well, my company sends you that email asking you to confirm your email address and, after you do, we send you the permission-based email newsletters on behalf of the website owner. We have signed up tens of thousands of independent sales people, entrepreneurs, network marketers, musicians, and non-profits all through word-of-mouth referrals. I got that one up to $72,000 a month in income and that was very nice. Here I am in my early 20's making seventy grand a month. That's quite a feeling.

I set my first real income goal at $2,000 a month. I remember it well because I wrote it down on a post-it note and taped it to my computer monitor. It was one of those really big tube monitors that take up half of your desk. It was yellow from age; I bought it used. That income goal set into motion a series of events that resulted in me making $72,000 a month. We all need to have goals. I said to myself, "If I can just sell 100 subscriptions at $19.95 a month, that will be $2,000 a month." With two-grand a month, I could pay all my bills. I could travel, take a 1 or 2 week vacation per year, and live job-free.

When I first started out in business, I didn't have the money to buy my first computer. I had to get a loan from a local bank and even that was somewhat of a hurdle because I didn't have credit.

I didn't have a lot of money when I started. I didn't have a lot of things. I was eating ramen noodles. If I had cheese and ham to cut up and put on the ramen noodles, it was a good day. I couldn't afford soft drinks; I had to drink tap water. You can only go so far on an income of $600 — $800 a month, right?

Then I had the stress of college. While in college, it was my goals that got me through by being intensely focused on them. I worked 12 hours a day, and often through the night, toward those goals and I started noticing some success along the way. I was achieving my goals and setting new ones. I was using my goals as stair steps to get me to where I wanted to go and, with each step, seeing a little farther ahead.

It's very important that you set goals. Write them down and date them for when you will achieve each one. Some will be realistic, others may not be, but still write them down. Even your unrealistic goals will become realistic with time.

Set some short-term goals of 6 months. Start out with small, easily-achievable goals. Maybe you want a new laptop computer or just a new cell phone? Maybe you want to be able to make double payments on your automobile loan or another debt you might have? What you don't want to do is to set too large a goal with too short a time table like paying off your mortgage of $200,000 in 6 months. It's probably not going to happen in that short period of time.

I have also started a couple of other businesses that were not network marketing businesses. With one of them, a wireless broadband provider, I broke even on the deal, and that was after three years of me working 80-hour weeks with it. In the other business, I lost about $50,000, which was nothing compared to the entire year of my effort, energy, and 14 - 18 hour days, 7 days a week that I had invested in it.

After those back-to-back failures, while on a Caribbean cruise, I was introduced to another network marketing company, the one that I am with today and building a worldwide empire. This is my 12th network marketing company!

One of the things I admire most about network marketing businesses is that your overhead is very small. This means that you can get into profit very quickly, sometimes in your first month of business! Compare that to a traditional business that typically takes three to five years to see the first penny of profit. It's no wonder most people fail at a traditional business; they just aren't set up to operate for 36 - 60 months at a loss. With network marketing, we don't have to operate at a loss at all if we hustle!

Doesn't it make perfect sense to take someone's blueprint that's already proven and follow it? I mean, if there are already people making money with someone's plan, the only variable is you, right? So you start at it and you may not be that good at it, but what if you work hard and get good at it? What if you learned the skills? What if you asked the right questions of the right people, and what if you started hanging out with the right people? Do you think these things would have an impact on your success? You can bet they do!

I used to have an ego problem. I wanted to own my own company, and each time I was in a network marketing company, I didn't see myself as the "owner." This limiting belief kept me from running wide open with my opportunity until I identified it, talked to several company owners about it, and laid it to rest.

When we join a network marketing company, it is our business — WE own it. It's not in the traditional scenario as one might picture, but it's in a scenario that I think you will find makes more sense for most of us who just want to run wide open at whatever we do.

Having discovered this to be something that has crossed the minds of a lot of leaders, I asked a few and here is what I found out. If you were to own a network marketing business, you would not be a network marketer! It would be just like any other business; you would be more like a traditional business owner or manager. You might as well buy a Subway franchise or build a car wash; it's the same thing. If you're the owner of the company, you're not going to have the same type of lifestyle as the top income earning distributor for that company.

## Build it big

I started out broke lower-middle class, working for someone else. I took what little money I did have, about $700, and joined my first network marketing company. It took almost all of that. I had less than a $100 left to my name when I started in my first network marketing company. I didn't have a lot of money. I was almost out of money, but I did have an incredible amount of desire and was very driven.

What I've found is that most people don't vacation that much. If you asked your friends who work a job or own a traditional business, I am willing to bet that you will be shocked to find out that very few of them travel every year. I mean, most of them probably only take one real vacation every four or five years. I wasn't happy with that statistic. I wanted to take a real vacation whenever I wanted!

I remember my sisters had these Cosmopolitan magazines that I would look through. On the back of one of them, there was an advertisement for the U.S. Virgin Islands. I remember saying to myself, "I'm going to visit that magical place someday. Someday, I am going to lay on that beach right there." I have been to the U.S. Virgin Islands many times with my family, and the dream started with that ad in the back of that magazine.

I used to cut out pictures from travel or car magazines and pictures of beautiful women that I would then tape onto my bedroom wall. You can probably picture in your mind right now the type of place where we lived, the type of place where it was acceptable to tape pictures on the wall. It was a lot different from the place where I live today. When you're a kid, you don't know if you're rich or poor.

I was happy, but I was sad a lot because my friends were getting toys like gaming systems, televisions, stereos, and nice cars. I was always told that we couldn't afford these things. I constantly heard my parents say, "Maybe next year," and, "We can't afford it." I decided as a kid that I wanted to be wealthy, extremely wealthy. I wanted people to respect me, and I wanted to help people create their own wealth through their entrepreneurial adventures.

My passion today is exactly that. I help people make the transition from working for someone else to working for themselves. Every day is different and I have the opportunity to meet and network with some of the most amazing people on earth. It is fulfilling for me to watch them make the transition. Who wouldn't want to be out here in the middle of the ocean with their friends making money and being happy?

One word of advice: when you're looking to make money for yourself, look at who you are and at your life first, then decide the type of lifestyle you want to have.

Do you have children? Maybe you want to spend more time with them — hopefully you do. If this is the case, then you need to be looking for something that offers a lot of leverage and maximum flexibility. I have two children and a wife. I need something that fits in around them, their activities, and our trips together. I don't need something that takes me away from them or something that takes me away from the home that I have worked so hard to pay for.

I have a very close friend who has to travel a lot with his job. He doesn't have the option. Either he travels or he doesn't have that job. He is stressed out a lot because of this, but it's not on his own terms. Make sure that you choose something that you can do on your own terms.

## Don't let your JOB dictate

Most people create their life around their job. Take for example someone who works a 9 to 5 job, five days a week. That person might as well just draw an "X" for those hours and days because they're not available. Their employer controls them, everything from the hours they are away from their family, to the type of car they drive, to the style of house they live in, to where they live, what they eat, where they vacation, and how often they get one.

Please make sure that you pick a business that fits in around who you are and what you want to do. There are a few businesses that you can do that with. I don't think you can do that with a franchise business or a traditional business because you have employees to manage and this usually requires you to be there most of the time, which means little time for your family.

With a network marketing business you still have responsibility, but it's a different type of responsibility. You can have the responsibility in the middle of an ocean on a cruise with your friends. You can take the responsibility anywhere you want to go, whenever you want to go, and with whomever you want to go. The network marketing lifestyle offers maximum flexibility.

Something else that I found is that you don't have to make as much money when you work for yourself as when you work for someone else. Now, I usually don't talk about this because it's not really a benefit, but it is worth noting in my opinion. I would never want to see someone start a business with expectations of making less than what they're making at their job. Your expectation should always be to make more because you can. If you don't consume more, just give it away. Give it to people who deserve it, give it to worthwhile causes that you are passionate about.

If you don't work for someone else, you don't have to leave your home. Think about all of the cost savings with this one. I was just talking today with someone on the cruise ship who was getting ready to sell their car. They just moved to a big city where they can walk, bicycle, or hire someone to drive them.

Just imagine if you didn't have a job and didn't have to commute. You would probably keep your car anyway, but you wouldn't be driving as much, which means you wouldn't be filling it up as often. You wouldn't have to buy that expensive wardrobe. When you work from home, you can walk around in your boxers or nothing at all. I wear a t-shirt and boxers to work most days and some days, just a robe.

## A formula for success

In network marketing, our inventory is our relationships. If you make your relationships your inventory, that's something nobody can take away from you. It's all about the people you meet and the connections that you make. We're friends now; we met on this cruise. It doesn't matter where I go, what company I build with, or where you go or what company you build with, we're still friends. Our relationship is still intact. So if your inventory is relationships, then doesn't it make sense to collect as many of those relationships as possible? You want to have a big inventory. So you build relationships with as many people as you can.

The first word in network marketing is "network." Robert Kiyosaki said, "The richest people in the world look for and build networks while other people look for work." If you have those relationships and if they're intact, I think you could be dropped out of an airplane onto a desert island with only your cell phone and you could build the business from there.

Something else a lot of new people get hung up on is that they join a company and like the products so much that they think the products are what will make them successful. They then try to learn everything they can about the products. A lot of these companies are nutritionally-based, so new distributors try to learn all about the ingredients, what these ingredients do, and what happens when they're mixed with other ingredients, product testimonials, and so on. People get caught up in all these details and it leads to inactivity.

The best use of your time in network marketing is talking with people, inviting them to presentations, presenting your product and opportunity, following up, and sponsoring them into your program. Your product is irrelevant, in my opinion. People join people; if you like me, if you know me and trust me, then there's a good chance we are going to do business together.

Build and nurture as many relationships as you can with people, including people involved in our profession. I know that when I first got started, I felt like everybody in other network marketing companies, and even the people in my company, were my competition. They are not.

## Your attitude

They say, "Your attitude is your altitude." I agree. Your altitude is most certainly determined by your attitude!

My number one attitude is that I believe everybody is an entrepreneur. I know this to be true because if you research the origin of entrepreneurship, you will discover that there was a time when 98% of the population, almost everyone, were entrepreneurs, and the 2% worked for them, not the other way around like it is today. It was during the time when kings and queens owned the land. They would lease the land to people like you and me, to entrepreneurs, who would do things with the land to create value. Maybe we would put cattle on the land and sell meat or produce cheese, milk, and such. Maybe we would plant corn and grow fruits and vegetables on our land. Maybe we would be bakers. Each had different ways of taking our land and creating something of value with it.

The kings would lease the land to the people and the people would produce something of value from their land and then pay their lease. Whatever they had left, they would live on. They would also barter, so if you had cattle and maybe I had fruits and vegetables, then I would trade some of my apples and carrots for some of your milk and cheese. Nearly everybody used to be entrepreneurs, so this tells us that most people are, in fact, entrepreneurs.

Success breeds success, poverty breeds poverty. If you grew up in a family of entrepreneurs, there is a high probability that you're going to grow up and become an entrepreneur. Likewise, if you grew up in a family where both parents worked at the local factory, you will most likely grow up with the belief that you need to work in a factory.

I expect everybody to be an entrepreneur. That's a very high expectation, I know, and a lot of times people will say to me, "You can't expect everyone to be an entrepreneur." But I say, "Oh, yes I can, absolutely I can!" Entrepreneurs create something out of nothing and everyone is capable of that.

## Lead generation

I recommend everyone use Facebook to generate leads. This may change in the future, and probably will, but right now it is a goldmine with upwards of a billion people spending time there. The average person on Facebook has over a hundred friends, so that's a decent sized network. I regularly see people on there who have hundreds, even thousands, of friends. People are spending a lot of time on Facebook. We can access Facebook in the middle of the ocean on a cruise ship, which means that you can use it just about anywhere. In fact, a third of Facebook's users access it via their mobile phones.

I use Facebook as my Rolodex. If I need leads, I go there first. Hopefully, you have an opt-in form where people can opt-in for more information about your business opportunity and/or sign up for your newsletter. Maybe you offer them a free report and build a mailing list that way. Maybe you use business cards or drop cards? I routinely leave a small stack of them at the cash register when I pay for gas. You may also include them with your tip when you go out and dine. Or maybe you meet someone at the grocery store that has a positive attitude, start a conversation with them, and then ask them for their contact information so you can stay in touch. Chances are, they will ask for yours, too, and that is when you should give them your business card!

There are a lot of places that have community boards. Places like Starbucks, Panera Bread, and usually grocery stores have community boards where you can put up tear-off flyers. I keep a stack of tear-off flyers in the armrest of each of our vehicles at all times for these occasions.

Another strategy I like to use are what I call my "silent salesmen." They are plastic yard signs that you stick in the grass at busy intersections. Make sure to check your local regulations first because some areas prohibit them, so be careful. Most places they are tolerated. I will risk a $3 sign being pulled up and thrown away for a few hot leads every day of the week! This method usually costs me about a dollar a lead to generate a voicemail saying, "Please tell me more about what you are doing; I am interested!" So that's a very good lead for a buck. Imagine what a thousand of them could mean to you in your business! That's something all of us can do — we can all use business cards, we can all use tear-off flyers, we can all use yard signs, and all of these methods get people to come to us.

I think a lot of new people initially fail because they pitch people. When you do this, you appear desperate. It is obvious and a major turn-off. The moment someone perceives you as being desperate, it is game over. People like to join successful people and successful people do not operate from a position of obvious desperation. It is okay to be desperate; just be mindful of the methods you use and the mind-set you have while building your business.

So you may be wondering, "How do I get people coming to me on Facebook?" For starters, be positive all of the time — not just part of the time, all the time. Here are some Facebook tips:

(1) comment on 10 people's statuses every day,
(2) comment on 10 people's pictures every day,
(3) send out 10 friend requests every day to people that are not yet involved in network marketing.

I prefer business professionals, such as real estate agents, because they're already self-motivated. They understand entrepreneurship and they are used to working on a commission.

Let's re-cap: 10 status message comments each day, 10 picture comments each day, 10 friend requests each day. When you do this, you're touching 30 people each day and that's almost a thousand people a month! Pay attention: a thousand people a month, that's 12,000 people a year. WOW! You're well on your way!

I also suggest updating your Facebook status at least 10 times each day. Say positive things that cause people to think and inspire them. Ask thought-provoking questions. Be controversial. If nobody comments on one of your statuses, you can delete it, right? Throw something else out there; you're just fishing, that's all you're doing. And eventually, you'll say something or ask something that catches people's attention and suddenly you'll get 30 or 50 or 150 comments!

It's all so simple, people want to get ahead. They want to make more money than they spend. They want to spend more time with their spouse. They want to spend more time with their kids. They want to travel more often. We all want to be happy. We all want to be loved. We all want to be accepted for who we are and we all want to feel significant.

Focus on those little things and don't worry about the 50 ingredients in your product or how much money your top income earners are making or how much your compensation plan pays or how it pays. Focus on people. We're in the people business. Network marketing is about people. It's about leadership. It's about personal development. People join people and they will join you when they like you, can trust you, and when they believe in you.

Spend the majority of your time working with people, creating and nurturing your inventory of relationships. As long as you have an inventory, it doesn't matter what happens in the future!

## Managing your time

I am able to accomplish more than most people because I do something and, because of doing something, I have more leverage. Some weeks I don't work at all.

There are a lot of people who are smarter than I am, who know a lot more about the business than I do. Some of them are in my down-line. They have all this knowledge and intellect. They read all the right books. They listen to all the right people. They attend all the right events, but they do nothing, so they have nothing. The reason that someone who isn't very knowledgeable, perhaps someone who just got started, has success is because they are doing something, an income-producing activity!

When I am building, I don't need to know everything about the company or its product line. As long as I am sold myself and I do something, I will attract other people to me. When you are positive and excited about what you are doing, your enthusiasm will attract people to you.

## Daily activities

I have a routine. My daily routine involves waking up, checking email, making coffee, eating breakfast with my oldest daughter before she goes to school and my 3-year-old who stays at home with me. She helps me make coffee, and then we do breakfast together. Right now, we practice the alphabet. Just very basic stuff, but it's the stuff that too many people miss out on with their own kids.

I check email usually before I get out of bed. With my iPhone, I can roll over, grab my phone, and check email right from bed! Then I walk downstairs to make coffee and spend time with my wife and daughters who typically finish sleeping before I do. After breakfast, I walk a few steps to my office where I shut the door and can sit there in thought as I send replies to the important messages I received earlier. After 30 minutes to an hour, I go play outside on the deck with my youngest daughter.

I think many network marketers spend wasteful amounts of unproductive time checking email, chatting on Facebook, and surfing the Internet. Before they know it, the whole day has passed them by. Even worse, they wake up the next day and repeat the same processes over and over. These people don't make much money. They have little success because they're not spending their time on income-producing activities.

There are probably 40 things that I do each day on Facebook if you count the 10 times I update my status. I actually automate that part using a special software application that you can get for free online. It allows me to simulate that I am online when I am lying on the beach or playing with my family. I spend about 30 minutes each day on Facebook with my 40-item routine.

This cruise has been a real test for me because I only bought the 100-minute internet package. Usually I buy four or five of the 250-minute packages. With this being a 9-day cruise, it works out to about 11 minutes per day. If I can build my business in 11 minutes a day from the middle of an ocean on a cruise ship, imagine what you can do!

I don't allocate a certain block of time for prospecting leads. I just fit it in. Whenever I am having an unproductive or negative day, I try not to talk to anyone. Our mood is contagious and I certainly would not want to infect anyone with a bad mood. I use my "down" days to ramp up my personal development. These are usually the days I read the most. Read until you are happy and positive again!

Sometimes people rub us the wrong way, right? Sometimes we're trying to be nice and sincere to people and they treat us unfairly or disrespect-fully. How do you handle that? Well, you keep your mouth shut and just go and expel that energy in a positive way by reading, get your mind off of it as fast as you can! You can have a great reputation, but if you say the wrong thing, it can be gone in an instant. Use those days to read books and limit your interaction with others.

The days that you're on top of the world or when you have had too much coffee are the days that you will want to get on the phone with people and you will want to get on Facebook because you're in a productive state of mind. You can knock out a whole lot of stuff really quickly on days like these. I found that when I'm having a good day, everything goes my way. Every single conversation I have is positive. Likewise, when I'm having a bad day, almost everything goes against me. Almost everything is negative. It just gets worse.

## Mentors and your success

Some mentors of mine include Jim Rohn, Zig Ziglar, Robert Kiyosaki, and Tony Robbins. Inside the profession, I listen to my up-line leaders. I also take advice from Tom Schreiter, Art Jonak, and Orrin Woodward. I have a special place in my heart for Dale Calvert because he was my first mentor. I really like Dale because we think a lot alike. He built a company to $125 million in sales, right up the road from me in Kentucky. He helped grow the company to 60,000 distributors and did it in five years. That's pretty remarkable! Dale created something out of nothing and was at a low point financially when he started his journey into network marketing. That's a commonality I have noticed amongst people who have created extreme wealth in their lives; they started with nothing but a dream.

Another person I know within the industry built a company to over $150 million in sales. He started with a $10,000 credit card advance. He didn't even have the $10,000 he needed to start his company, but he was able to borrow the money to start and ultimately built a $250 million enterprise.

Some people will use their current financial situation as an excuse. They will say things like, "I am broke. I don't have the money, and my credit cards are maxed out." Rich people make excuses too. They will say things like, "I am too busy. I don't have the time." These two excuses are perhaps the most popular two excuses we hear in this profession. When you get one of these two excuses, understand that it is because of what you said during your conversation with them. Chances are, you said too much or you attempted to be the tool instead of using one.

Maybe the person is money-focused, but all you talked about was helping people. You might as well have been speaking Chinese! It is important that we spend a few minutes getting to know our prospect so that we can identify their personality type and then speak to them in THEIR language.

One of the most empowering things I have come to discover in this business is that most people who have had success started with nothing. They started right after the death of a loved one. Or they started right after a bankruptcy. Or they started right after a divorce. Or they started right after a mid-life crisis. Or they started right after losing their job. They almost all started with nothing during what they will tell you was the lowest point of their life.

I think this is important to note, because some people will say, "That person is successful because they have a lot of money. They must have been born into a wealthy family. It must have been easy for them, because they probably had a lot of money to start their business with." That's all false. Successful people are successful because they are driven by a vision that is larger than them. They are goal-chasers, they do something, and they persist.

— Shannon Denniston

# FROM ZERO TO MILLIONS STRATEGY

· Create a daily routine for success.
· Lead Generation: Facebook, Yard Signs, Tear-Off Flyers on Community Boards, Business Cards, Drop Cards
· When you're looking for a way to make money, take a good look at your life right now, what you want to change about it, and then find the type of business that will give you the lifestyle you want.
· Be positive all of the time. Inspire people by sharing your lifestyle with them. Be controversial, be a thought-provoker!
· Build your inventory of relationships, both with people inside and outside our profession.
· Follow my 40-item Facebook routine daily.
· Focus on creating and nurturing relationships.
· Do something.

# CHAPTER 5

# THE TOMATO SEEDS

My name is Juan Carlos Barrios. I was born and raised in Mexico City, Mexico. About 20 years ago in 1990, I learned about this industry.

I am a professional musician and I studied to be a musician in school. I learned to play the piano and the violin. I knew that when I became a musician, I would probably never be rich or make a lot of money. I was okay with that. I wanted to be happy and I didn't mind if I was poor. I told myself, "Well, at least you are already poor!"

I was 22 when I was introduced to network marketing. I thought originally that it was not for me because I am not a salesperson. I am not a talker either. I was very shy and was spending a lot of time playing my piano. I did not have a lot of friends. I just didn't think that the business was for me. The first time I learned about it, I said no.

But then my friends brought me to a seminar. In the seminar, I saw things differently. With the business, I could not only learn to make money, but I could learn to be a leader and become a better person. I could also develop some skills to learn how to be successful. The seminar was interesting for me because, before that, I never learned about how to become successful. I really liked the person who was speaking. He said that when he started he was shy and he thought that the business was not for him. He seemed to be a lot like me. I thought, "If what he is saying is the truth, then I can make it in this business."

I started my first business and I met with my first mentor. She came to visit me and said, "Juan Carlos, you can be big in this business." I believed what she was saying. But then I learned that she said the same thing to everyone. But, it showed me how important it is to help people to believe in themselves and what they can do. Words can change your life.

I started to look around and I found a man who I wanted to be like. I started to ask him questions and learned from him that really there are just two secrets to being successful.

The first secret is to never quit. Never quit. It will take some time, because it depends on finding the right people. But the first secret is not to quit! The second secret is that you will never have success in business if you are not a success as a person. You need to keep growing and learning. You need to read good books and go to seminars and listen to inspirational tapes.

You need to do the things that you are learning. I found out that when I did these things that I was learning to become a better person. I was learning to be a different person. I listened to a very interesting tape and I believed what they were telling me. I learned to believe in myself by being around the right people. When I think correctly, I can do things the right way.

It did take a while though. It took me 7 years to grow my business. I was very young, I didn't know a lot and I wasn't thinking correctly. I wasn't around the right people. No one around me wanted to join the business and the few around me who did decide to join me didn't stay with the business. This was because we were all kids. We were all around 20 years old, all musicians. So it really wasn't the right environment to build a business. But, I had learned that I shouldn't quit so I kept going. I kept following instructions and learning and every day I tried to sponsor one new person.

I can tell you that after 20 years of being in the business, I am very rich. And it is great! I can also tell you that I have a lot of people who look up to me and people that will join the business just because I say so. They want to do things just because I am who I am. I think to myself, "Really?" Twenty years ago, no one wanted to be in the business and no one cared to do what I was doing.

What happened? It happened because of the person I have become. I understand that and I realize that I have to keep growing and keep learning because of that. I need to do this because I have to help other people to grow and learn. In order for this to happen, I need good training skills and good leadership skills. I need to help more and more people.

I have been in three different companies. All of them were very successful. However, I don't believe that you become successful just because the company is successful. You can play tennis with a good tennis racket, but that doesn't mean you will win the game. It is the player, not the racket that wins the game. That is the key.

I think of myself as a musician, but being a musician, I had nothing to offer my wife and my kids and the world. Being a musician is a great thing, though. I have friends now that are professional musicians and I think, "I do not want that for my life." It is funny, though, because now I drive a nice car, have a splendid home, and I travel all over the world. I have a very enjoyable lifestyle and I have people who look up to me and they want to be like me. I just spoke to a friend and she is now in the business and doing well and she said to me, "I understand this now." Her husband is also in the business.

I was giving a seminar a few months ago in Monterrey, Mexico, and I saw that the crowd of 200 was mostly young people. I asked how many were less than 20 years old and a number of people raised their hands. I said, "Let me tell you my story."

I told them about how I started my first business when I was their age and how I was so afraid. I told them that I was shy and I was afraid that I would not be successful. I told them that when I started talking to people about the business, no one wanted to join. I told them that it upset me. But, because I did not quit when things were going wrong for me, I succeeded. So, never quit. You may get upset because you do not see your group growing and you do not get a big check right away. Sooner or later you will. Sooner or later, you will become a better person and learn how to build your business.

Recently, I had a conversation with my 16-year-old daughter. She was talking with me and I realized that she was using all the positive and encouraging words that I am using. All I could think was, "My God! I am rich!" These are the things that money cannot buy. It is so important to teach your children these things.

People get frustrated because they don't see this. They only see that the check that they want is not arriving. But they are growing in many ways and learning things from the business that cannot be sold or bought. You are growing in many ways in your life, but you don't realize it because you cannot see it. But your children do see it. They live with you every day and they are watching you as you go about your day. They are learning things like how to follow your dreams and how not to quit. These are important things. This industry is incredible for that reason. I just love it.

## Handling slow downs

Back then, as things began to happen, the business slowed down. Then, I'd work on building the business and it would slow down again. But you have to keep building it constantly. I would build, build, build, and then I would stop. I was expecting my people to grow my business.

Let me share with you one of the first big mistakes I made. As soon as I got 5 people sponsored, I felt like I had made it big. I felt like those guys were going to build my business, but I wasn't spending any time developing those guys. They never did anything. But I spent many years waiting for them to do something. I would wake up every morning and say, "What will those guys do today? What is wrong?"

But what I understand now is that not everyone is going to be able to build a business right away. So if you want to build a big business, then you need to keep sponsoring new people and building your business all the time. It took me 7 years to understand that. As soon as I understood the need to sponsor new people, things fell into place. It was perfect. So I learned that I was spending time with the wrong people. I was expecting them to react when they would never react.

I have another story I'd like to share with you. My daughter was 3 years old and she saw a pack of tomato seeds at the store one day. She wanted me to buy the tomatoes seeds for her and she said, "Dad, please buy me these seeds." My son, who was 4, said, "Dad, buy me some seeds, too." So I bought them each a pack of seeds and then we went home.

We went into the garden to prepare a place for the seeds and it was painful for me to make this garden! We prepared the soil and I helped the kids. I put the seeds in the ground and we watered them. My kids loved it. Each pack of seeds had about 40 or 50 seeds in the pack and I thought, "Oh my God — can you imagine all these plants!" Our set up was about one square meter and I thought, "Well, we will see how many come up."

Do you know what? Only 2 tomato plants grew! And I said, "What? There were over 100 seeds. Why did only 2 grow up?" But it is the same with your business.

You may plant seeds in the hearts of many people, but perhaps there are only 2 people who are ready to start a business. The rest of the seeds have the same land, the same water, the same soil, and the same care. Everything is the same, but why did they not grow? No one knows.

That is the way of life. But it is a good thing to realize that if you want a huge return on your work, if you want a big business, you need to sow a lot of seeds.

My work every day is to plant seeds of success in many people. Sooner or later, one person in my group will understand it and they will begin to grow. But, not everyone is ready to grow. I spend most of my time with the ones who are ready to grow. The rest of the people I still care about and I don't treat them any differently, but I cannot spend a lot of time with them.

## Leapfrogging

One of the things I have learned is this concept called "leapfrogging," that you can get a large jump in the business once you do certain things, and I have had many leapfrogging moments. Some of them might have happened after I finished a book. I remember the first book I ever read. I began crying after I read it. I began to call my people and I started to use the things I learned in that book. I took immediate action. I jumped from one level to the next level. It went very fast. And then nothing happened for a while in my business until I went to hear this speaker.

I was attending conventions and seminars, and there was one speaker that shared the same story that I was living. He had found a sponsor and given that person 100%. For 7 years, nothing really happened in the business for him. And it was the same thing with me. For 7 years, my business stayed the same and then he told me what to do in his speech.

When I learned what to do, I took immediate action. I repeated exactly the same thing that he did and it was like, "OK. I know what to do now." It took about 6 months and it all worked out. I got 10 checks in 6 months just by using what I learned from that one speaker.

So you never know what will happen or what you will learn. You need to do it all — the seminars, the cruises, and the CD's. You never know what you are going to learn. I think the third one was when I met this man who spoke at a seminar and I read his books. He really challenged me to grow. He is an incredible man and he brings out the best in people. He is a very strong person and is incredible on the stage. He's very good at speaking and always challenges me. He has lots more money than me, but the only way to learn to make money is from someone who has made more.

I learned something important from a close friend who just passed away who did very well in business. He told me that no matter how much you are making or how well you are doing or how successful you are and how many wonderful things people say about you, never forget.

You know, you get to talk on the stage and have people ask you for autographs and people want to take your picture and all. But you should never think that it was all you. It is the teamwork that made success happen for you. Realize that you never would have made it without your team.

So never stop learning and growing. Keep sponsoring and sharing this opportunity all the time.

## Daily leads

I do it the old way. I started in the business 20 years ago! Back then we didn't have computers and we didn't use terms like "lead generation" and all of that, you know. Basically, I believe that people join your business because they know you and they trust you and they like you. So I always sponsor people I know.

But, then again, if I don't know them, I get to know them. This is easy because I make friends very easily. Then it is easy for them to want to become a part of my team. To begin with, I ask my friends and then I ask the friends of their friends. I teach the other people in the business to also do this. Right now, after 20 years, I realize that I now have a lot of people in the business! I know many, many people. So after you have been doing this for 20 years, you will realize the same thing. After 20 years, you realize that the people who have been with you for a long time have really improved over the years. They are different now than they were 20 years ago.

For the new person, friends and family are a good way to begin. They know you and trust you. They like you and, because of this, they are a good place to start. And then get to know their friends and their friends.

I also use another old way to generate business. I teach them about the business and use the training system. I use seminars and books and CD's and all of that to learn and grow. Growth is important. If I sponsor a person, I give them tools to grow. If I don't give them tools to grow, they will do nothing. They do not know how to run a business and so I have to teach them how to run a business. The system can really help you to do that and to teach people how to become good leaders. Every company has a system....a training system. Use it.

## Never quit

Normally, your very close friends and family never join the business. Never. Especially family. No one in my family is doing the business. Maybe some friends joined the company at first and then they quit. In the very beginning, I remember 20 years ago, when I first started, they were very skeptical. They told me that it was stupid and crazy and that it was a scam. I was so influenced by the tapes that I was talking the same way and they said that I was being brainwashed. I was angry when they talked that way. I was very angry at them.

But you know, now after 20 years, well, I've changed my mind a little bit. First of all, when someone tells me no, I respect that. It takes courage to say "no." They need courage to tell me that. So I don't take their answer personally. I know that they are not saying no to me personally, they are just not ready right now to take action. Maybe it wasn't my best day to present them the idea. Maybe it wasn't a good day for them. So I never take it personally.

The other thing is that I just don't share the business with people only to get sponsors. This is not my main goal. My main goal is to become a friend. Really, whatever happens is OK.

I'll tell you a story that illustrates this. I was talking to my friend 2 days ago. He is an old friend from my first company. I was actually in his down-line when I started. I was one of his leads. I found leads for him then. And we spent an hour talking about a lot of things and we had this incredible conversation.

At the very end of the conversation, he asked me what I was doing now for work and I told him. He said that it is wonderful and that he heard only wonderful things about the company that I am with. It was a problem for me because he is my good friend and he's not doing as well as I am. I wanted to say to him, "Come and join with me!" One day I hope that we can be working together. I really hope. But you know what he said at the end of our conversation?

He said, "Juan Carlos, I am so happy for you and I am so happy where I am, but just in case that would change, please send me information about your company." You never know what will happen in the future. Sure, I will send him the information, but he doesn't need to join or look at anything. He just needs to remember that he is my friend.

So my goal every time that I speak to someone is not to sponsor them. If you have a friend, you have a leader forever. Do not try to turn their "no" into a "yes" and make people feel uncomfortable when they have already said no. After that, the conversation will go really badly and your friend will not want to talk to you anymore. Your friendship is destroyed.

There is plenty of time and there are plenty of people. So if one seed is not ready, don't push the seed to be ready. Just plant the seed. Keep up the friendship. If you know that I care about you, you know that you are important to me.

As far as reactions, if there is someone who has a reaction, I understand that. And I never, never argue. I understand their position. I respect that. Then, they know that I care about them and we become friends and maybe down the road he will decide to join the business. Maybe now is just not the right time. You never know what will happen if you wait 6 months or so.

Let me tell you this: if your family does not want to do the business, you need to respect their decision. Big time. It is important. Understand that not everyone has the same goals. Not everyone wants to be a doctor or a musician. It is OK and it is a good thing. You only have one family: one mother and one father and there is only one you. You are an individual. So if you become a millionaire and you can take care of your entire family, then they will have to join the business. It becomes more convincing if they can see your success.

Everyone will struggle in the process, but let me tell you something: we cannot blame other people for our lack of growth. If you are trying to grow and no one is helping you, the information is out there. You need to go and find it for yourself. People will be more than happy to share if you ask. If you go on the internet, you can find lots of information. You could spend years learning it all. If you go to the library or the bookstore, you will find that there are lots of books about marketing and personal development.

Like I said, the information is out there. So, we need to understand that we cannot depend upon the up-line or our company for information for our own growth. It is our journey. And you can learn from people who aren't even in your company. So don't complain, just try to learn. If you are looking for answers, like I said, you will be happy because the answers will find you. Remember that you will find whatever you are looking for. If you are looking just for fun, you will find that too.

I realize that whatever happened in your life makes you the person that you are today. Reality is shaped by our physical world and also by our inner world. What we think influences our reality. Our thoughts determine our focus. If you focus on death or problems and negative things, that is your focus and you aren't going to grow. You will be negative. If you focus on success and being a better person, you will be focusing on positive things.

In the business, we call it "the maturing of souls." The big check that you get doesn't define who you are: your inner thoughts define you. Are you positive or negative? One step at a time, these things change you. If you read good books, listen to inspiring CD's, and join cruises like this one, you will learn. Do a lot of learning and help people just starting out. Even if you don't want to change or aren't trying to change, you will change. Change is natural. Success is natural. It is a part of human nature. To be successful, we have to put ourselves in an environment where we can grow. These are the things that are crucial to our growth and our lives.

## Mentors are everywhere

I have had many, many mentors. I will tell you that I consider every single speaker to be a mentor. Every single speaker that you listen to on this cruise is a mentor. Perhaps they just give you one or two phrases and you think, "I understand now! I was blind before, but now I can see. I understand it now." Maybe it is a book that mentors you or a CD or a phrase. There are many things. Maybe it is a speech. In fact, I can tell you that I honestly cannot name all my mentors. There have been so many. I cannot remember every single person or every single thing.

## Belief in self

We need to understand that belief is a very strong idea. If a person has a belief, it means that they think it is true. That idea is true if they believe it, whatever it may be. I think it is a process. You can't change beliefs magically, but it is a process. Little by little, if they are exposed to good stories and testimonies, they will grow.

If I take them to inspiring events like seminars, their belief will also grow. Say I take them to a seminar on Saturday. That following Monday, they will be talking to their family, their friends, their boss, and it goes down the line. Perhaps they will say, "You know — my brother-in-law was in a company and lost everything," and this affects their belief and it goes down. It is a process.

If they begin to sponsor people, their belief grows a little bit up; then they get a large check and it grows; then they sign more people up and it grows even more. But then they get upset and their belief goes down. For some it is a process that sometimes goes up and sometimes goes down.

But, he has to realize that he has control over the process. He has to think positive thoughts and he has to do the work because, my friend, no one can influence you unless you want to be influenced. If everyone tells you that this won't work, and you believe them, well, just think about it. What if EVERY single person he met was telling him negative things like, "You are crazy." But suppose he made it anyway. He can do it if he believes he can no matter what anyone says. You need to understand that if you are going to build a business, you need to believe in yourself, and if you have that belief, then nothing in the universe can stop you. I think it helps people if you bring them to the events and expose them to the books and CD's and the system. That is why the system is in place. To help you succeed.

You can bring someone into the system, then the system will take care of them. You are not only leading people, but you need to encourage them and tell them that they can succeed. And even if you just sponsor one person, you are a leader. You are sponsoring one person, but you are leading them, too. Encourage people! Make it a habit to encourage people. Keep telling them good things like, "I know you can do it, you can do it. You can make it! That speech was incredible. You dress so well!"

Encourage people. Encourage them a lot. Remember what I told you at the beginning of the interview. Say things to people like, "You are the best. You are the next leader. You are the next manager." If you encourage people, you will be successful because people will want to join your business to be with you. If you tell them that they can do it, they will believe you because they trust you. So your words are very, very powerful.

## From beliefs to actions

I don't waste my time. Don't waste your time. There are many things that will waste your time. The internet can really waste your time when you do things like chat, read emails, or read junk mails that you do not even have to read. There are also a lot of people that need constant attention. But they will never do anything in business or anything else in life. They won't accomplish anything, but they will take up a lot of your time in the process.

Because your words are powerful and encouraging, a lot of people will want to be encouraged. But, there are people who need to be encouraged 24 hours a day, every day! They never accomplish anything. They take all of your time and your energy, but they never do anything. Be careful of people like that. Take care of the friends you have and spend time with them. But watch who is around you. Watch who you are spending time with and how you are spending your time.

Be careful of the television, because it can easily waste a lot of time. Maximize your time. We all have 24 hours a day! Use it wisely. You can make calls using 3-way calls. This way, you can talk to many people at the same time. You can talk on the phone in your car or listen to CD's while you are driving. Use your time efficiently. But, do not spend too much time on the phone. It is important to be organized and to do things as fast as you can.

You need to make about 20 to 30 calls a day, each day. You need to do at least one business presentation per day. When I say at least, I mean that you can do more than one. There have been days where I do 7 or 8 business presentations per day. You should also spend some time listening to inspiring CD's. Remember, this is just when you are starting. Sooner or later, you will become successful and then you will spend your time solving problems. This is why it is so important to know how to solve problems with people. Right now, 95 percent of my time is just dealing with and fixing problems. But, you know, they pay me to fix problems. This is what I get paid to do.

## Prospecting

How much time you spend prospecting depends upon your business. If you don't have enough people to sponsor, you will spend most of your time prospecting. After a few months, you won't be prospecting so much, but you will need to do follow up calls and promote the next step. But it depends on a lot of things. It depends upon what is happening in your business. Initially, it will take a lot of time to find sponsors. And things will go really well for a while, but you still need to keep finding sponsors. You need to spend time training and following up with your people and you will see that you are spending a lot of time training.

Right now, after 20 some years, I get probably 2 or 3 prospects per week. Once I begin to get friendly with someone, they usually join the business. It is different now, because I might go for a week without sponsoring anyone and then one day I might sponsor about 3 or 4 people just in one day. But for many days, I might not sponsor any people because I am working with my people and training them. If I am busy with my own group, I don't worry about getting leads.

It depends what is going on, really. I use Facebook only for getting new prospects. I do not use it for anything else but prospecting. I put status updates on Facebook a lot. Sometimes I open my Facebook and I have 5 or 6 people who are saying, "OK, please tell us more about your business." So I might spend one day prospecting on there if that happens.

## Daily routines

Let me tell you how things usually go. I wake up around 9 am when my body tells me to wake up. I don't use alarm clocks because I don't like them. Then again, I don't have a job, so I really don't need to use one. I usually wake up around the same time as my wife, so we come down to the kitchen in our pajamas and eat breakfast which is prepared by our housekeeper.

My office is in my house, so I cross the garden from the kitchen, and there is my office. Of course, I have an assistant in my office. My assistant is usually in the office when I get there around 10 a.m. This is still early, so usually my secretary is dealing with issues and taking calls so that I don't have to answer them at this point. My secretary also creates files and material and schedules meetings and trainings. You know, sometimes I go to the office in my pajamas! When I get to my office, I respond to a couple of emails and I might make a few calls. I then go back to the house to take a shower around 11 a.m. and then head back to my office. I might dictate some notes to my secretary about a presentation.

I just love to do that. My wife and I say that we will exercise every day. We keep trying to do this, but so far we haven't had any success. After that, we go to pick up the kids at school around 1:30 p.m. This is fun to do together. Then, the housekeeper usually makes lunch so we can all sit down to eat together. The housekeeper cleans up after us as well. We have a lot of help around the house, which is wonderful. After lunch, I make several calls. I do a lot of that. I use the phone a lot. Sometimes, I play with my kids in the afternoon. I just bought a PlayStation for the kids and sometimes we play together. Other times, we watch movies that the kids are interested in. My kids like to watch movies with me.

I probably work about 7 hours, or maybe 8, because I am building a new company right now. I have been with them about 8 months. Every day we have at least one presentation during the night. Presentations can be in different places. Sometimes I take my car and come back home late. Once in a while, my wife goes with me to a presentation and we go to the movies afterward. I love going to the movies. Also, right now I am writing a book. Some nights, I might answer emails and then take some time to write a little bit in the book.

As I said in the beginning of my interview, I am a musician, so I prefer the night time to the day time. I like to stay up some nights until 2 or 3 a.m. in the morning just practicing music and playing my piano or violin. Luckily, I have my piano in a room far away from the rest of the house, so it doesn't bother anyone. I love music and, if I am in the mood to play my instruments, I play.

I am also very passionate about my team. I am always thinking, "What can I do to help them? What else can I do to help them grow?" So you have to hurry up and write your book, because I think it will help a lot of my people!

People say to me all the time, "You have been doing this for so long. Why are you still working? You should be slowing down. Haven't you achieved your goals yet?" Recently, someone asked me that question and my answer was that it is human nature to accomplish more and more. There is no limit to our desire to accomplish as much as possible. There is no limit, really. This is simply what I do and what I love to do. This is my job and it creates direction and meaning in my life. It creates a purpose, so without it, my life would be empty.

It is not about me and my family and all. It is about my leaders. It gives me a lot of joy to help them. I think I will never stop. I will always be doing this. I can't imagine stopping my work doing the business. I think that this is for me. This is what I do and I love to do this. This is why I will never stop doing this. I enjoy my life and this is part of it. Maybe I will stop right before I die or maybe on the day that I die. But I don't want to stop, really. I don't need to stop, either. This is so much fun. How can you call something that you really enjoy doing a "job?" Sooner or later, you realize that you are not in the business; the business is in you.

— Juan Carlos Barrios

## FROM ZERO TO MILLIONS STRATEGY

· Don't ever quit.
· Attend seminars and cruises.
· Associate with people in the industry.
· Respect people's decisions whether or not they want to join the business.
· Remember the story about the tomato seeds; not everybody is ready to join the business.
· Encourage people and empower them.
· Don't waste your time on television, junk mails, and the internet.
· Keep sponsoring and recruiting new people
· Take full responsibility for your own personal development.
· Listen and read inspirational materials everyday.
· Remember the tennis story: the racket doesn't make someone talented at playing tennis; it's all about the player himself.
· Imagine your mentors as bricks; each individual brick is necessary for building the house (business).
· Make a least 20-30 phone calls a day.

# CHAPTER 6

# PAINT THE WALL IN ONE COLOR

Hi, Nikita, tell me your story. How did you get into network marketing?

I started a long, long, long time ago. I remember I was young and handsome at the time.

In 1993, I was running my own traditional business and I was looking for ways to increase sales. I was attending seminars, listening to the advice of coaches and business instructors who I thought would be able to help me achieve my business goals. It worked. I was able to increase my sales and at one point in time, I had 5 stores.

I attended a Life Spring seminar which was all about building your self-esteem and improving your leadership skills. It was a 3-day seminar and, at the end of the seminar, a guy came up to me and he said, "Hey kid, I can see you are an intelligent person. I would like to introduce you to a new business."

Intrigued, I said, "What's that?" And he said, "I'm talking about something that I started myself." I said, "Can you just go straight to the point? Don't waste my time!" He said, "Okay, the business is finding new people. Teach them what they need to know to run a business and you get a commission out of that." So, for me it was like a dream come true because I was always looking for some kind of business where other people were working for me while I could collect a commission from their work.

It's called leverage, but I didn't understand that concept or know the term at that time. This was my first introduction to the world of network marketing.

I know, after 18 years in the business, that this guy was a newbie himself at that point. He didn't know what to say; he didn't know what to do; and he was scared of me. But, I am thankful to him, because he was convincing enough to get me interested in what he was saying. He was also confident enough to approach me. I've become more tolerant now, but back then, I was very opinionated and very assertive.

So, anyway, that's how I got involved in network marketing. I found that I really liked the industry. I started reading different books and, at that point, we didn't have anything in Russian. I didn't know any English at that time. I had to have people translate what I was reading into Russian. There was no internet available because it was 1993. Now that I look back, I realize that it was a difficult time, but at that point in my life, I didn't think so.

There is so much information available now. When people complain that they don't know what to do or what to say, they have no excuse. They can find information on CD's, DVD's, or on the internet. Nowadays, it is easy to find information about network marketing.

## Success grows
I've been in this new company for a little over a year and I have over 600 sponsors. I don't think that it's a big deal or that it means that I'm

a huge success. What it means is that I have a stable base and that my company is growing. For me, that is what it is all about — building the business and making it a success.

I think my experience and the skills that I learned in my previous venture really helped. I was in the previous company for about 12 years. So it's not like I am just constantly jumping from one thing to another. I'm not someone who thinks that the grass is always greener on the other side of the fence, because I know that it's not always like that.

When I was a child, my father used to say, "Nikita, if you want to be successful, you just have to paint the wall in one color." I was probably around 10 years old at that time and I said, "What? What are talking about?" He said, "You know, don't worry. Sooner or later, you will understand what I mean." About 10 or 15 years later, I realized what he was saying.

We have so many distractions in our lives. We try to do too much at once. The key to being a success is to do one thing really well. That is why it's so important to be focused. If you're a carpenter, be the best carpenter in the world. If you're a networker, be the best networker you can be! Work with one company and pour all your energy into that venture. Don't just give up simply because it looks like something isn't going to work out at first. Usually that just means that you lack the skills necessary to make it work. Usually it isn't the company that is not working, it is you. It might be because you don't know what to say or when to say it.

I believe what's most important for people to be successful is for them to develop leadership skills. Charisma is also important, because most leaders have a lot of charisma. If you don't have charisma or leadership skills, you won't be successful.

## Change is required

I hide my aggressiveness a little bit better now. Of course, now I am very wealthy. I wasn't when I first started. But I have learned to tone down my aggressiveness when I need to tone it down to get things done or to work with people, but I am still the same person at heart. I've learned, too, that it's all about numbers and leading the people I prospect. I am the leader; they need to do what I say and when that happens, my down-line will succeed.

If I could go back in time and still remember everything I know now, what would I do differently? I would never ever work with a company that has a management program with a Soviet kind of mentality. In most cases, these companies never achieve much. Yes, that is just my point of view. Also, a lot of these Soviet companies have a much more aggressive mindset. That doesn't always get you the results that you want in business. If you have ever been to Russia or the Ukraine, you can understand what I am talking about. People on the streets don't smile at all. Usually, they seem to be in some sort of trance. If you smile, people think you are stupid. But, that is really what they are thinking!

That is why I would never work with this kind of company. The second thing is that they really don't consider what works in the real world. They say they do, but they really don't. I say this because they do not consider distributors as the main source of their income. They think that distributors are their slaves. They try to play games and show the distributor who is in control.

This doesn't help your business to grow at all. If you are open-minded and you have a different opinion, these types of companies will start pushing you to get rid of your beliefs and opinions and to see that you are wrong and that they are right. That is not good.

I know that if I would want to change companies, I would go to a company that manages things more along the lines of the way that the United States-based companies manage things. These companies usually work better and achieve more.

When you are thinking about which company to join, you need to consider four important issues. First of all, you need to look at who owns the company. That person should have a lot of experience in the network marketing industry. They should also have experience as a distributor. Most people think they understand the industry because they have read books and attended seminars. That is great, but they don't really understand the business. You gain experience by doing! That is the only way that you will ever really understand this business.

The second important issue to consider is how much support the distributor gets from the company. For example, there are times when you will have questions that need to be answered before you can get your business started. This will happen a lot, especially when you are first starting out. If it takes a month or so to get an answer back, it is really going to slow down your business growth. Building a business is really like building a relationship.

If I ask a question and it takes a long time to get an answer, I may get upset. Then we are back to square one building the business because we have to deal with the problems that we are having with communicating. This will have a negative effect on our ability to grow our business. For example, if a prospect asks a question and you ignore him or her, that person isn't going to be likely to be motivated to do a lot of work within the business. If a prospect wants to know the answer to his or her question, we have to deliver that answer as soon as possible. Otherwise, it can be bad for the business and for our relationship with the prospect.

The third thing to look for is the system that the business has in place. If you ask the leaders in most companies about their system, they will just say, "Yeah, we have a system." But when you really begin to ask them questions in order to learn more about their system, they don't want to get specific. This is how this industry got a bad reputation. People don't want to give answers to the questions. Watch out for companies that get upset if you say something negative about their leaders and then they tell you that you just have to be more positive or that you must read their books or listen to their CD's because you are so negative. Maybe these techniques worked 10 years ago, but they don't work today.

Network marketing is a real business with a lot of rules. There are also different systems. It is really important to keep learning. Learn the latest marketing techniques that are available. Learn, and then use, what works best for you. Whatever works for YOU.

And the last thing that is important to consider is how will this product or company be viewed by young people? I call young people who are 20-25 years of age "Generation Y." It is important to select a product which young people in this age group will find attractive, simply because most MLM marketers do not think to include these people on their prospect list.

Generation Y is largely untouched by the MLM industry. Sure, some MLM companies will say that they have a product that appeals to this age group, and they will say that they have a lot of young people in their company, but this isn't really true. When you look at their company statistics, you can see that it is not the truth. Anyway, from my perspective, these are the 4 critical things that you should look for when you are considering joining a company.

## Marketing tools

I'm a big, big, big fan of databases. The best advice I could give to anyone considering having a career in this industry is to build up your database with good contacts. Most distributors spend about 80% their time on a daily basis giving out product information and discussing the compensation package and not a lot of time doing presentations.

If you spend all your money and time doing this, who is going to do the presentations? I believe, like the Japanese people say, "It's much better to spend more time on planning in the beginning than starting off doing something right away without a plan."

I would recommend that you try not to do it all at the same time. Pace yourself. Spend 80% of your time doing presentations and perhaps 20% of your time building your database and making contacts. Over the years, I've learned lots of ways to build up a database. What method you use depends upon the country in which you live, your personality, and the particular situation. Some methods work better in certain situations than in others. Have a variety of methods that you can use in a variety of situations.

One technique I use is to talk about myself. Usually, I tell people about how I didn't speak any English when I came to the United States. I wanted to start building my database in this country, so I just memorized a really simple sentence and then I started calling different organizations. I used to be a professional swimmer when I was young and I decided to give it a try again. I started going to swim lessons. I found a group called the "American Association of Senior Swimmers" and I got to know some people there. Then, I started building my database just because I don't believe in making "cold calls."

These people are good to start with because they have similar interests and habits. For example, if you work or used to work in the airline business, you can use the same technique. You can go talk to the people who work in that industry. Even if you don't know anybody there, you will say, "Hey, I'm a flight attendant too." Or, you can say, "Oh, I used to be a flight attendant before," and right there, you have a connection. How do you do it? You make some kind of introduction and, once you have made the introductions, you can start asking questions in order to find out more about your prospect.

Your conversation might go something like this:

> "Hey listen, you probably know that a lot of people nowadays take vitamins and minerals on a daily basis because we don't get enough in the food we are eating." You then ask them if they take vitamins and they will tell you their experience. Usually, people take some sort of food supplements, whether it is vitamins or minerals. So, usually I say, "Hey, listen, I have some really good information about that. I just came across a very big product that I'm using myself and I would like to recommend that you use it as well."

In most U.S.-based companies, they offer a 30-day money-back guarantee. So, there is no risk; the risk is zero. Just try the product and if you don't like it, you can return it to the company and get a full refund.

So, get your starting point: something in the past, your profession, your habit, sport, or some kind of activity. Begin there and you will find a lot of people like you who you can talk with about your product. And it's really easy — you can apply this technique to any kind of profession.

I personally do not like calling cold leads. It takes a lot of time and effort. It drains your motivation because you get a lot of rejections. Whereas, if you find people that you have something in common with, it will be easier to find prospects and get sales.

It's very simple and it is easy to repeat the technique. It doesn't cost you anything, especially with the internet. I would recommend to those people who speak really poor English like I do, for example, that you work on leveling the playing field. Work on your smile or being a warm, caring person. Make sure your charisma and personality come through when you speak.

You can offset the bad points with good points and you can balance your ups and downs. You look at your ability to speak English, or whatever language, and your charisma as a package. Then, it will be much easier for you to attract people to yourself. This is important, because people, as we know, do not buy the product, they do not buy the compensation structure, but they do buy you. It's a simple rule and it is the number one rule in network marketing.

## When English is your second language

Remember that any weakness can become a strength. For example, if your English isn't so good and you are speaking to a person who speaks fluent English, they will have to pay careful attention to what you are saying in order to understand you. They have to focus on you. That is exactly what we want.

FROM ZERO TO MILLIONS

You want people to listen. The 2nd thing that will help you is the fact that they will never forget you simply because they usually do not come across a lot of people who speak broken English. When you call them to follow up, they will recognize you right away, especially if you have the beautiful accent that I do.

You convert your negative points into positive ones. Then, you get people to listen to you.

## Using social media

A lot of stuff on the internet, I believe, is written by people who have never done network marketing. They want to sell you a dream, basically. They want you to believe that all you will do is sit at home in front of your computer and click a button and that's it. Boom! And all you have to do is just collect the checks. But, it is not like that. If you use the internet as a tool for your network marketing career, you have to remember that you will be competing online with huge corporations.

Before, they were using mass media: newspapers, magazines, radio, and TV. Right now, they use the internet, as well. Of course, they have big budgets; they have career salesman working for their company because they have enough money to hire them. If you start competing with them for your network marketing prospects, I don't believe that you are going to win that game. Even if you do win in the short run, you will lose in the long run. You cannot duplicate online and the idea of network marketing is duplication. If you can't do this, you have to be working all the time to earn an income.

Network marketing is all about residual income. There is none of this in internet marketing. Maybe a few years from now it will change, but I don't think so. The key element of network marketing is communication — personal communication. Newspapers, radio, TV, and the internet aren't personal. Yes, network marketing is a communication business and the internet is a tool for communication. We can use internet as a communication tool to provide information to prospects, but at some point, you have to meet them in person anyway. Otherwise, it's almost like "virtual sex."

## For the beginner

First, I would recommend you be in personal contact with your sponsor on a daily basis. Make it a habit. Wake up and call you sponsor. If you can't do that, meet your sponsor in person.

Second, you have to read for at least one hour a day. I believe that reading a paper book is important because it creates a connection. You hold the book and you have a connection. It's like when you go to the gym and you do certain exercises, your body gets stronger. It doesn't work that way when you read on the internet.

Third, you have to build your database. Call people from your database together with your sponsor. One of the biggest mistakes most distributors make is that they forget about the first two rules. So, if they call somebody, they should have their sponsor with them. You can do this using a 3-way call.

For the beginner in network marketing, I recommend *Your First Year in Network Marketing* by Mark Yarnell. Dale Carnegie also has a lot of different books on self growth. When I was young, I remember I had a hand written copy from my father. He gave it to me when I was about 10 years old. This kind of literature was illegal in Soviet Union, so it was a handwritten copy and it was passed from one person to another.

## My mentors

I don't want you to think that I am the best in the world. I just don't have one mentor. I have several different people including Tom "Big Al" Shreiter, Richard Brooke, Art Jonak, and Ken Seto. Ken Seto is my favorite. Ryan Pampas, he's not with us right now on this cruise, but he was here a couple of times. He is a great friend of mine who lives in California, right next to me. There are other people too.

I'm starting to keep in contact with them and get information from them. I called it solving the puzzle. Each piece of information is like a puzzle piece. They fit together and create a finished puzzle. Sometimes, they don't know that they're giving me information to help me. For example, you may be talking about an entirely different subject and all of a sudden I think, "Oh! I was thinking about this for the last year and you know how to complete the puzzle. Here is the missing piece."

Yes, I prefer to have personal contact with people. That is why I've been on the cruise every year for the last 11 years. I like attending because of the wonderful, skilled people full of positive energy that are here. I get that for free. That's a key word — FREE.

## Good habits to foster

I prefer to go to the gym as soon as I wake up. I work out for a couple of hours, and then go back to my home. Then, I make a few phone calls. That's probably it. I have a simple routine. Then I can take my car and go to the beach, ride a bike, read some books or spend time with my son. This is the way it is when I'm at home.

When I'm away, it's a little bit different routine because, mostly, I spend my time with my distributors. I might have 10-15 meetings a day where I just try to squeeze the time and make something happen much faster.

## Accomplishing more

I just do simple things on a daily basis. If you just call a few people every day, you are going to be way ahead of most of the people. Make a few phone calls everyday. Have a few meetings every day. I also believe that it's important to be positive all the time, no matter what. It's important.

My mom and my sister, they're really negative. They think in a negative way all the time. Those problems that they see as a big mountain in front of them, I see as a little piece of nothing. Let's just go over and forget it. But for them, it's huge. They have to discuss and talk and think. Even then, it is impossible for them to let things go. It's boring.

I hang out with a lot of positive people all the time, and if I have a nega-tive person or group of negative people, I just do my best not to talk to them at all. Negative people are like vampires. They suck your energy all the time.

For those who are a bit shy, but really want to go into network marketing, I would recommend a few different things for them. First of all, read books, as I said before, on a daily basis. Listen to positive CD's. In other words, use these things to affirm positive information to your brain by reading, listening, and viewing positive movies.

Secondly, build a database. Divide your database into different sections. One of them will be people with good communication skills. So, let's call that database the "database of leaders." If you're shy, it's really diffi-cult to attract people to yourself and your business. That is why I would recommend that you use somebody who is from your up-line or maybe your down-line, whom you feel comfortable working with in order to help you to attract leaders into your organization. In this case, your helper would be able to kind of squeeze the time and get results faster than you would. Of course, you need to work on building yourself as a leader.

Most people would say when they hear that, "This Nikita is stupid. He is out of his mind." Why would I help somebody from a side leg to build his business? I usually say, "You probably don't get the idea of network marketing because you have to think long term.

Let's say that today you work in a company called A, but tomorrow that company disappears or terminates you. Then, what will you do? Where will you turn? You will go to people for help, probably people that you helped in the past, and they will help you. You might say, "Oh my God! My company is the best of the best. I'm proud of it because it's the best of the best." But tomorrow, imagine the owner of the company decides to sell the company to a venture capitalist and those new owners just start doing crazy things. What your owner of the company was doing for the past 20 years or so, boom! It is gone. You already lost your connec-tion with the owners and the company.

When I say that, I mean trust in the company. If you lose that trust, you cannot recruit the company or promote it and its product. Then, your compensation starts to shift. Sooner or later, you will be out of the company because you left or because they pushed you out.

Think long term, not just 2 or 3 or 5 years ahead. You have to think 10 years, 15 years, 20 years ahead. You have to help a lot of people around you because they are like orphans. They've been signed up by somebody, somewhere and that somebody just dropped out. In any company, this is very common.

## Staying active

Some people lose their passion or energy, but were they truly leaders to begin with? Honestly, I wouldn't call those people leaders in the first place, because a leader knows how to motivate himself. There is a big difference between internal and external motivation too. If I am motivating you, you won't be motivated very long. I am an external motivator. A leader is internally motivated. That is why I wouldn't call this person a leader.

Secondly, if we are talking about a distributor, I would recommend that this person read books, talk to positive people, listen to positive CD's, and watch positive movies. These are big sources of internal motivation. But you have to work with that as a muscle. For example, if you go to the gym once a year, it's not going to help you much.

It's the same thing with positive thinking. Our brain is a muscle that works the same way with negative and positive situations. Whatever you trained your brain with, that's how it's going to work. I don't have any secrets. I don't have any unique, ingenious ideas.

## Driving force

Freedom is my driving force. I'm free to go anywhere and free to do whatever I want everyday. I'm free to decide whatever is going to be next. It's really, really, really important to me. I get invitations from different businesses and I do get new offers on a monthly basis. Some are really interesting, but in most cases, I would have to give up my freedom.

People like to see me as a manager of a big company, or a CEO, or some politician. But in all those cases, there are limitations. You can lose your freedom. Do you understand what I am saying? There is no way I want to lose my freedom.

## Words of encouragement

Think big promotion. Go to my website, nikitagromyko.com. When somebody comes to me for help, whether he is a newbie or whether he has been in business for 5 years without much success, I can't just say to him, "Hey, be positive and read this book." Sometimes that advice just doesn't work.

That is why I have a tablet with 64 different questions that are usually asked of me. When somebody comes to me, I usually say, "Okay, let's take that question and break it down." It's like doing math, because we see the problems and we work to solve them in a way that is workable and can be duplicated. I want that person to understand the problem and the solution.

If that person comes for help again, I can get his file and we can go over it again. Then we will see that this person didn't really understand or really didn't know how to fix the problem. Each solution and each problem will be unique to that person. It's not like a universal remote. Remember that movie with Adam Sandler? There is no such thing as universal advice, I believe.

Most motivational speakers have a solution that fits all kinds of advice packages because they make money out of speaking on stage. We make money out of different things. That is why if I give my distributors universal advice, it's not going to work for everyone. Then, I'm not going to get my residual income. What's the reason for me to even open my mouth and try to give bad advice? You see the picture? That is why

I mentioned my website, because there is no such thing as a last word from me. I could talk forever on this subject.

I would prefer to sit down with a person over a cup of healthy energy drink or tea and just talk forever. But we would talk personally about unique advice for this particular person and the particular problem they are facing.

## Dealing with problems

Ten years ago, I came up with this tool because I was frustrated with people coming to me and telling me their problems and asking for advice. It was frustrating because, in most cases, they were telling me the middle of the story and I didn't know the beginning of the story and I also didn't get to see the end of the story. But they wanted advice! How can I give advice when I don't know the entire story? I'm not a genius, a psychic, or a magician.

If you tell me the problem, I need to know the whole problem to give you a good answer. But in most cases, when you just come off stage, you don't have that time. People begin to ask different question like you are doing now. They ask for good advice before the end, before the execution, before the guillotine comes down and it is the end.

But, I would usually say, "Listen, here is my email. We have all the time in the world. Here is my phone number. If you want to get real advice, let's get together over Skype. I'm going to send you a file for the table which you are going to have to read. Look at that table. I'll look at my copy and we'll fill out the form together and discuss your problem." After about 30 minutes to an hour or so we will see the problem. So I am just reasonable. I'm not a genius or anything.

Secondly, I was personal. I wasn't trying to give universal advice in order to get rid of that person and ignore the problem. I gave advice that was duplicable and workable because we reached that answer together. That is valuable for the person who asked the question. It is kind of like I didn't give him a fish to eat, but instead I took him out on a fishing trip and we caught the fish together. Now he knows how to fish.

And also it saves a lot of time for me because most people don't contact me. They say, "Yeah! We're going to call. We're going to contact you." Then they disappear. So, in other words, the question was foolish or there was no interest from their side to get the real answer. This way, I can tell who is really interested and who isn't. It wasn't like I set up big barriers for them to contact me either. I gave them lots of ways. They could call, connect through Skype, email me, etc. It works.

— Nikita Gromyko

## FROM ZERO TO MILLIONS STRATEGY

- Build your database.
- Join communities where you have common interest.
- Guidelines for choosing a company:
    — Who owns the company?
    — Do they have experience as a distributor?
    — How much support does the distributor get from the company?
    — Is their system in place?
- Spend 80% of your time doing presentations and 20% of your time building your database and making new contacts.
- Develop your leadership skills and charisma.
- Read a minimum of an hour of motivating inspirational books, but a book rather than the internet so that you "get a connection."
- Associate yourself with positive, successful people.
- Become a leader who is internally motivated.
- Think of your business in the long term, 5-10-20 years ahead.
- Help other people in your down-line or cross-line.
- Do simple things on a daily basis.
- Become a master of what you do.

# CHAPTER 7

# GETTING STARTED RIGHT

To begin with, can you tell a little bit about yourself and how you got started in network marketing?

———

I started in 1994, although I was originally introduced to the concept of network marketing around 1990. I just didn't realize that it was network marketing.

I used to be a Houston broker and, during the financial crisis, I made some terrible financial decisions. I lost basically everything. I had about $300,000 in debt, with about $60,000 in debt just on my credit cards alone. Basically, I was looking for something. I didn't realize back then that it was network marketing.

You could say that I sort of fell into the business in 1994 through a friend of mine. I thought it was a unique concept because I could run my own business and I could help other people build their businesses while I was building mine. The concept of a residual income was very attractive to me. Shortly after I began, I joined another company. I've been with them since 1994.

In 1997, I realized that I had been introduced to this business in 1990. I bought products from a friend, but he never told me it was network marketing. If only I had known back then! I got involved in this business at a time when I was in financial straits. I was really struggling and looking for something.

To achieve a reasonable level of success, it took me about a year. I was making about a thousand dollars a week in the business. So that was about $52 thousand a year, and this was 16 years ago.

## Looking back

Knowing what I know now, I would have done a few things differently to achieve success faster. I would have planned my business a little bit better. This is no different then when you run a traditional business. Basically, you need a business plan. Network marketing is still a business.

But, a lot of times, people get involved in this type of business and they don't make a business plan. They have no plan, but they just have raw enthusiasm. They don't keep track of their business, either, to see how it is doing. You need to keep track of these things and have a system.

The second thing that I wish I knew at the time would be when to cut people off. For example, I would not spend too much time with the wrong people. You've heard this from others, I'm sure. Some people join the business because they want to have a distributorship. Others just join for themselves. Don't spend a lot of time babysitting the wrong people.

The third thing I probably would have done differently was to put more money into the business. The more you put in, the more you get out. With business, it's all about what you can keep in the end, not about what you make. Let's say you make 250 thousand a year. That's a lot of money, but if you spend 275 thousand a year, you'll be broke. These 3 points are my key points.

## Getting growth

To accelerate growth, it depends on how big an income a person wants to build within his business. The early stages are the most expensive time because you are taking money and reinvesting it into the business. Now if you don't reinvest, the money may not grow that quickly. However, some people are content to make an extra one or two thousand dollars a month. Some people want to make that in a week, and some people want to make it in an hour. So obviously the amount of resources that you want to put into the business will vary depending upon your goals.

Now, the challenge that most networks are going to have is that when they run into problems as they grow and mature, they will be short on resources financially. That is when it hurts the most. Figure out what you will have to pay for income taxes and plan to save at least 10-20% of your income. Then, add another 10% for incidentals or unplanned expenses. Then you can determine how much you need to make. You can definitely be frugal or do things inexpensively. You just have to be smart about it all.

I think that the key for people is to realize that this takes time and that they should not give up. Many of us are raised that way; we are born quitters. It is easy to say "I don't want to do it; I quit" when things gets tough. It really takes a person with a very strong will to stay in a business like this and to stay the course when things get difficult.

The second thing I think has a lot to do with whom you spend your time. That is the challenge. Think about it — when you were growing up, weren't your parents concerned about who your friends were? Of course they were, because your friends have a major impact on you.

141

I'll give you an example of this. When I grew up, I lived in a part of the city that was somewhat rough. I remember there was this one kid I used to hang out with during elementary school. One day, my mother said to me that I shouldn't be hanging out with this young man because he was a very bad influence. I didn't think so at that time and said, "Mommy, he's just a friend, it doesn't matter!" She was firm about it, so I didn't hang out with him. Years later, in high school, this young man ended up in jail. Obviously, my parents saw something in this young man that I didn't see as a child.

The reason I'm bringing that up is that we tell our children to be careful, but as adults, we don't think about the friends that we hang out with. There might be people who we, as adults and as network marketers, should probably not be spending our time with because they are not a good influence on us. So that also affects our attitudes, too. Know who your friends are and don't quit. These two key points will lead you to success in this business.

## Handling negative people

A negative spouse is a big problem. Unfortunately, that's why a lot of marriages break up — because the two people are going in separate directions. It is important to find out what the negative spouse is really concerned about. Is it that they don't believe in the business? Do they not like the industry? Have they had a bad experience in the past which is causing them to be upset?

Find out what the problem is. It could very well be something as silly as they're worried that their spouse will become very successful and that they would not want to be married anymore. It is important to address the issue and to find out why they are afraid of their spouse being successful. Spouses need to be working together. It is important that they are on the same page, because if they aren't, it can be very difficult.

## To be successful

People really need to develop the correct attitude. Next, I think that they need to do some work and come up with a business plan in order to have a realistic expectation about how long it will take to be successful. Most people who quit this business do so because they want to put in a small amount of time but want to earn a large income in a short amount of time. That is unrealistic. The challenge is that many times a prospect or the industry may not give a realistic expectation of how much work it takes. This is why people quit.

They have unrealistic expectations and when those expectations don't work out, they get upset and quit. I think it's very important to have a realistic business plan. You need to sit down with the new person when they first start and you need to go through the whole thing. The whole thing, as in how much time do you have and how much money do you want to make? Also, how long a time will it take to reach the goals that have been set?

For example, "Richard and I want to work with you on this business, but here's how it works. I bring the expertise and the experience in this business and you bring credibility with your prospects. You also bring the cycle that will bring big profit to the company."

Now, you have told your prospect upfront that you're willing to support them in their business, but that you will not do their business for them. You will do presentations and you will do tours to keep people interested. If they take one step, you take one step. If they stop, you stop. You do not want any distributor to ever feel that they can blame you because you did not support them or you did not build it for them. You're there to help them build their business, but not to build it for them.

It is important to set this framework from the very beginning that it is their business and that they are responsible for the success of their business. I think when you do that, you will find out where you stand.

The reality is that a lot of times people get involved in network marketing as a distributor, but they never should have been a distributor. They really should have been a customer of the product rather than a distributor. Unfortunately, most people who are network marketers automatically assume that each person that they bring in should automatically be a distributor. Then, they get frustrated when these new distributors don't perform.

Another thing to consider is that when you help your distributor build their business, you want to help them find someone to join their team as soon as possible. When people first join, they have about 3 weeks of raw excitement. They are enthusiastic and you want to help them make things happen. Ideally, you need to help them sponsor someone in those first few weeks. That should buy you another 3 weeks of excitement. If nothing happens in the first 21 days, the interest level will begin to drop off rapidly. Another, even more important thing, is that you want to find quality people that you can work with long term.

## Lead generation

A lot of times I work through the network marketing profession to find other people who have network experience. I tell them I might need a person and ask them to join me. Then I ask them about their up-line and who is at the top and how I can get in touch with them. Then, I contact these people. That also shortens your learning curve in terms of getting people on board. In the very beginning, it might be a little more difficult, because you're new to the profession. But, as time goes on, you will be able to attract people.

When I first started, I didn't have any experience, and it was difficult. You have to start somewhere. People tend to think that successful people have always been successful. The truth is that they started at the beginning just like everyone else did at one time. Of course, with anything new, there's always a lot of work in the beginning.

Do I advise beginners to make a list of 100 people and start calling them? Absolutely. I would not get them to call them by themselves, though. I would probably have the up-line or the person who brought them in make a 3-way call with them. That way, they will have someone who is more experienced with them.

I would have them make a list of their top 10 prospects too. The top 10 would be people who have experience and networks already in place. Those are the people on the "chicken list." I probably would not call these people first, only because you are so new. You need some level of experience to begin to talk with them. So talk to the other 90 people. The new distributor needs a little bit more experience in talking to people before they come and talk to the people on the "chicken list."

The chicken list is the top 10 out of 100 on your list. This would be the group of people that your new distributor thinks very highly of, but whom they're scared to contact.

## *Personal development*

I read a lot of personal development books. That really helped a lot. I was quite involved in personal development even before I went into network marketing, so those principles really helped a lot. I also have a lot of mentors in the industry that are not necessarily from my company. They are in the industry, though. They help me and keep me focused along the way.

In addition, having a good schedule set is a great idea. Ideally, new people should be seeing prospects or talking to prospects every single day. They need to do that full time, every single day. Sunday is usually a good night to set an appointment with people personally. Sunday night is also a good time to contact people to set appointments to meet them during the following week.

I would probably do training on a Saturday. I try to do something locally every Saturday. With people who are further away, we could set up a full training call or a webinar. This way, people can bring in others at any point in time and they know that they are going to be properly trained. The training calls or webinars can also be on Saturday mornings. It comes down to training. Now I plug into North American conferences during the week with the company and I also do recruiting conference calls once a week. The key point is to just stick with it and learn about the company. It is so important to do this so people will want to stay.

You want to create a habit of doing a little bit of work every single day. That's when the success happens — when you keep working at it. You have to have discipline to be successful in this business. Unlike regular work where you have set hours, in this business, you are on your own. You have to be disciplined so that you can set your own time schedule. Otherwise, the day will go by; the weeks will go by; and you haven't had much success.

## Masterminds

I have people that I talk to who are generic. I call them generic because they're not involved in my company. These are friends that have been with me and known me for a lot of years. I keep in contact with them and we give advice to each other as well as feedback.

I also do the same thing with my group. We usually have a weekly conference call where we touch base with the key leaders and discuss how the week went. We talk about what went right, what went wrong, and what we need to do differently. Then, we do some planning for the following week in terms of setting goals.

I believe in weekly team calls. At least give your team a call once a week. You really have the chance to touch base with people you know right away. One thing I learned about this business in the last 16 years is that this is a personal business. The more you talk with your team, especially those who are really working, the more they will appreciate you for it.

## Overcoming shyness

How to help people overcome their shyness is a challenge. I talk to them and find out whether or not their shyness has disabled them. Has it affected their life in terms of getting ahead? When it comes down to it, if they really want to make a difference in changing their life, then they have to make adjustments for that.

You know, when I first started in this business, I was very, very shy. It was very hard for me to talk to a lot of people. But what tends to happen to introverted people is that the more successful you become, the more outgoing you become as well. It is more of a confidence thing. My goal is to help that new person get some success early on because once he has success, confidence will come with that. Then it just gets better and better.

Success then brings confidence, then the confidence gives you more success. I would also recommend they read *How to Get Rich* by Felix Dennis. He's my favorite. Another one is *The Slight Edge* by Jeff Olson. And the third is probably *The Richest Man in Babylon* by George S. Clason. I've read a lot of books, so it is hard to narrow it down to just three.

## Leading forward

I'm really an advocate of goal setting with the leaders. I work with them and then I find out if they are archiving their goals. I check to see whether their plans are realistic. When they reach their goals, we set new ones. Sometimes, for example, people make it to a pcint where they're making more than they really want to and they don't want to take it to the next level. You need to plan for that.

Some people think that their "why" has to be part of something big. Some people want to save the world so to speak. Others don't want to.

For example, when I first started in the business, I was struggling financially. I just wanted to put food on the table. Once I was able to put food on the table, then, of course, my goals changed to the next level.

For most people, I think they're beginning to find out what's important to them when they join the business. Once they get close to their goal, they set the next goal. You should always be setting new goals in your business. It's crucial.

## Getting started

I really believe that the start of your career is important. You need to get started on the right foot. You need to be told the truth and you need to know what the expectations are for the distributors, as well as the sponsors. Be prepared and have a plan in place. Set short-term and long-term goals. Until a person is ready to really saddle up to work this as a real business, they will only have a hobby.

I'm sharing this with you because when I first started, I didn't have this. I saw that if I had done it in a different way that it would have been better. I would have seen results faster. I've seen up-lines tell people anything they can just to get them to join.

You know, getting people into the business is the easiest thing to do. The work really starts after you get them to join. Unfortunately, many people have the mindset that all they have to do is get people to sign up. Those people also give our profession a bad reputation; they only care about signing someone up and then they're gone. You never hear from your sponsor again. You're not there as a recruiter but as a sponsor helping them to grow and develop themselves.

— Ken Seto

## FROM ZERO TO MILLIONS STRATEGY

- Have a business plan.
- Keep track of the business.
- Have a system.
- Invest money into the business.
- Save at least 10-20% of your income.
- Add another 10% for incidentals or unplanned expenses.
- Don't quit.
- Know who your friends are.
- Develop the correct attitude.
- Help people in your down-line sponsor at least one new person every 21 days to keep them excited.
- Associate with network marketing professionals.
- Sunday is usually a good night to set an appointment with people personally and to contact people to set appointments to meet them the following week.
- Create a habit of doing a little bit of work every single day.
- Discipline yourself to be successful.
- Practice goal-setting with other leaders.
- Set short-term and long-term goals.
- The work really starts after you get them to join your business.

# CHAPTER 8

# WE ARE THE PRODUCT

I t was apparent from the first few seconds of our conversation that Bonnie and Robert are like two sides of the same coin. They are yin and yang. They were created for each other and they definitely complete one another. On top of the great husband and wife relationship, or precisely because of it, Bonnie and Robert have together made millions of dollars in network marketing.

But, it was not always that way. Over 20 years ago, when Robert started, he struggled and had a debt of $101,766.71 from his attempt at network marketing.

His very first customer was Bonnie and, despite her slim build, Robert managed to sell her weight-loss products as part of his network marketing business. At first, Bonnie was a skeptical non-believer of the MLM business. She thought it was crazy that Robert thought network marketing would work!

But Robert saw a vision. Very simply, Robert saw that some people had done what he wanted to do and he believed he could do it, too. So, he jumped in with both feet. Cynthia Kersey, author of *Unstoppable*, says, "Believe in yourself and pretty soon, others will believe in you."

That is precisely what happened. Despite the lack of results in the beginning, because of Robert's belief in his vision, Bonnie started believing, too. And it's a good thing she did, because together they accomplished great things. Robert is the vision guy and Bonnie is the detail person. Robert is a good starter and Bonnie is a great finisher. They complement each other in the business. They really are the network marketing yin and yang. And, once they supported each other, magical things happened.

Robert grew up in a family of successful businesspeople and self-made millionaires. Early in his business life, he made the crucial decision to leave behind all the "Country Club Smart" ways of his business upbringing and pursue something different, something more challenging, something exciting. As he puts it, "I woke up one morning and realized our family business had too much family and not enough business. It was simply time to make a change."

Robert grew up in his family's business with every expectation of someday running the show. After all, his family founded the high school award cheerleading jacket business, which was in its third generation in an ever-expanding market and Robert was the oldest son! Robert's future seemed certain as he worked in the business part time throughout college and then joined full time upon graduation with a business degree.

But, like most best laid plans, reality intruded on the blueprint for Robert's success. Robert was repelled by the corporate politics which he knew existed in most businesses. And, Robert did not want to be ruled by the expectations of others, which proved to be the deal breaker.

He wanted to break free of the dictates about when he had to work, how long he had to work, and when he could take time off. Robert was fortunate to recognize early on that there had to be a better way. He wanted to earn money to live the lifestyle that he knew was possible without having other people's rules etched in his soul.

In October 1984, he got involved in a home-based business with the intention of being able to replace his income from his job at the family business within 3 to 5 years. While Robert learned a lot about business on his own, he also incurred quite a bit of debt which derailed the "better way" he had envisioned.

Robert's goal in life was to be a no-limit person. After hearing Wayne Dyer's tape, "How to be a No-Limit Person," Robert realized that he had been creating limits in his life. "I've tried to become a no-limit person. It started me on the path to what I've become today."

Robert went into business for himself after realizing that Corporate America would not allow him to live the kind of life he wanted. "There are so many limitations. They expected you to work so many hours per week and handle a lot of politics, which I didn't like, so I started searching for an alternative way to have the freedom I wanted, a career that would enable me to experience life the way I wanted to live."

He is now well on the way to realizing his goal, having been named Distributor of the Year from MLMIA for two straight years. He says that one of his heroes is John Glenn, who inspired him — another no-limit person.

Robert's path in network marketing has not always been easy. When he first started in this business, he went all out but lacked the proper mentorship to become successful. But, Robert did not set limits on himself or give up on his dream. "I never gave up on the vision of the kind of lifestyle I could live through this business. Four years later, after finding the right kind of mentorship, I was able to clear up all my debts, walk away from my job, and devote myself full time to my career in network marketing."

Having the right support system in place is crucial to success in any business. As shown in Robert's career, it made all the difference in his level of success. He says that the best thing about being self-employed is that he gets to make his own decisions. "The people I meet and work with are enjoyable and I'm able to make a difference in their lives. That is the greatest pleasure imaginable.

But, as those who know Robert know, he's not a man who gives up on his own or other people's dreams easily. Despite the early setback, Robert never lost sight of his vision of what it would be like to live life on his own terms. He knew what his terms were: to not have to worry about money, to be able to wake up when he wanted and not be tied to the call of an electronic rooster, to take a 30-step walk to his office to begin his day, and to play basketball — his passion even now — on a regular basis. In his mind's eye, he knew his future involved world travel and making positive differences in the lives of those he came into contact with.

Robert took a big step toward making his vision a reality on September 7, 1990. On that day, Robert left the family business forever and began to focus 100% on helping others accomplish the financial freedom he enjoyed. Like many who have taken that giant leap, it wasn't easy for Robert in the beginning. But he was determined, and that determination paid off.

Prior to being interviewed on a stage, an interviewer asked them the question "What is your product?" Both of them immediately replied in unison, albeit it was not rehearsed, "We are the product." They looked at each other and laughed.

## Why people join your network marketing business

The truth is, you are the product. You are the reason why people join your network marketing business. "This is the reason why I am a strong advocate of personal development," says Robert. In fact, Robert himself teaches network marketers around the world how to develop themselves and succeed through his book *Street Smart Network Marketing*.

One of the books Robert recommends is *Outliers: the Story of Success* by Malcolm Gladwell on the importance of spending the time to master one's field. He also likes the book *Influence* by Robert Cialdini because he believes that this business of network marketing is nothing but influencing others.

He said, "The key in this business is to make people see things from a different perspective." However, he prefaces this statement by saying that you have to realize first that there are people you can influence and people you cannot. As to who those people are whom you cannot influence, Bonnie shared her frustration of wanting to help everybody. But eventually, she realized that she cannot want for others what they don't want for themselves. Those people without the drive, without the dream, without a strong enough "why" are simply people whom you cannot influence no matter how hard you try.

## Mentor plus FOCUS equals a Mercedes

One of the breakthroughs in Robert's network marketing career happened when he met Robert Natiuk at an MLM convention. Robert immediately got Mr. Natiuk as his mentor. His new-found mentor told him to FOCUS on one network marketing opportunity and really commit to it. Robert followed his mentor and, from January to November of that year, his business grew so big that the company gave him a Mercedes Benz as a reward!

He attributes his phenomenal success to his mentor's advice to FOCUS and COMMIT on the current network marketing business. From his third year on, he has never earned less than $100,000 per year, but has earned upwards of a million dollars!

Robert now shares his wisdom as a mentor, speaker, and communicator to those who, like him, want to live life by their own rules and have the financial security he enjoys. He is often invited to speak at network marketing and internet marketing industry event always with the intent of reaching as many people and businesses as he can so they too can succeed as he has.

In 2008, Robert served as the Chairman of the Elite Network Marketing Congress in Singapore, showcasing the global reach of Robert's mission. He has also released two tapes: "Getting Started in your Networking Business" and "The Secrets of the Money Funnel and How it Can Make you Rich."

## Join the right company

The company you choose to represent will be the vehicle to your success and financial freedom. So, when choosing a company, be as cautious as you would be when buying a real automobile. The company, the product, their marketing resources and tools should all have integrity.

Find a company that sells a product that you could love and that is so good it sells itself. Choose a company that has such great marketing tools you could easily duplicate and literally 'plug-in' or a company with a duplicable business system. And, of course, the company should pay a juicy amount of commissions.

## Find a mentor

Every successful network marketer should have a whole bunch of mentors, trainers, or coaches. Network marketing is about duplication! They can help you avoid the mistakes they once made in the past and help you stay on track as you move on. Mentors are valuable resources for new ideas and approaches. Communicate often with them. Successful mentors will always be happy to help because your success is their success too.

## Change your mindset

It's all in your mind! If you believe that you can make $10,000 per month, then you CAN! Networking mentor John Milton Fogg calls these "habitudes" or habits of attitude. In his book, Robert explains in detail the powerful "habitudes" for network marketing. In order to be able to "do and have" what you want in life, you must first "be" the kind of person you want to become.

## Set your goals

Goals are tools to keep you focused and help you become more and more determined to succeed. Be specific when writing down your goals. How much money would you like to earn in 1 year? 2 years? 3 years? After writing it down, put your goals everywhere, so you will be able to see them all the time.

## Dedicate your time and effort to your team

Network marketing works differently than a conventional business. In a conventional business, you work for a boss who works for his boss, and his boss works for his boss and so forth. In network marketing, your focus and dedication should go to your team, the people you lead, because they joined you. Whatever you are planning to do with your business, do it for the sake of your team. Your team's success is your success. And even with an excellent network marketing company, your up-line's success will be your success too.

## "No" is not a personal rejection of you

There will be numerous people saying "no" to your business. Don't take it personally. Some people do not have the big picture about becoming free or about the unlimited opportunity that network marketing has to offer. No matter what you say to them, they will just never say "yes." Make sure that you spend your energy only with those who share the same big picture with you. These people should be your target.

There are five types of people you will find in network marketing:

1. People who want good products at a fair price — customers
2. People who want to have their products paid for
3. People who want to replace a current payment
4. People who want to replace their current income
5. People who want to become wealthy

If you want to have your products paid for, find five customers.

If you want to replace a payment, find five people who want to have their products paid for.

If you want to replace an income, find five people who want to replace a payment.

If you want to become wealthy, find five people who want to replace an income.

WOW! At first glance, we thought this two-part "Rule of Five," though brilliant, was way too simple.

So we did the math.

Let's assume your company pays a respectable 30% commission for retail sales and a respectable 20% for down-line commissions. For each customer buying 100 points (about $150) per month, that's $30 per month to you. For each down-line rep or customer buying 100 points per month, that's $20 per month to you.

If you want to have your products paid for, find five customers. That's 5 x 30 = $150 and your products are paid for. If you want to replace a payment, find five people who want to have their products paid for. You'll have 5 + 25 = 30 people in your business, earning you 30 x $20 = $600 per month. Now you have your products and your car paid for! If you want to replace an income, find five people who want to replace a payment. You'll have 5 + 25 + 125 = 155 people in your business, earning you 155 x $20 = $3100 per month, or about $37,000 per year. Most people would regard that as a good income, or at least a start on retiring early or bringing a spouse home from work, sending the kids to college, or putting a new roof on the house.

If you want to become wealthy, find five people who want to replace an income. You'll have 5 + 25 + 125 + 625 = 780 people in your business, earning you 780 x $20 = $15,600 per month or $187,000 per year!

## Getting serious

When you are serious about building your multi-level marketing business, training your down-line is crucial.

One of the best tools for training the people in your company how to succeed in their business is teaching them to learn the business by heart. A good system for learning the business is repetition. You know that when you hear a song many times, it sticks in your mind and you begin to remember it without even trying. If you like the song, you will probably even sing along with it.

Learning your business can work the same way as learning a song, but the rewards are much greater. There are many different ways to learn about how to succeed in network marketing. You can use online training tools with e-books, forums, blogs, articles, newsletters from your company, and other learning opportunities on the internet. You can also find lots of helpful information in books, magazines, tapes, CD's and DVD's. Three-way telephone calls, coaching classes, and teleconferences are helpful for people who would rather use the phone than the internet.

One of the most effective ways to learn your business by heart is by attending meetings and seminars. You can start the process for your down-line by holding small informal meetings in your home or at their homes. If you have a few people in your organization, conduct weekly business briefings and make them interesting and informative. Devise methods of creating an incentive for your down-line to attend the sessions and reward them for attendance. Serve snacks and occasionally have potluck meals for them and their families. Give door prizes, have contests and try to make the meetings fun. If it is possible, get a consultant from one of the best companies in the industry to speak at a seminar to teach the people in your group how to sell products and about prospecting and the recruitment systems. When these things are explained to them by a knowledgeable speaker, their sales should increase and their recruiting efforts should be more fruitful. They will learn the best ways to promote their businesses and answer questions that their prospects ask.

Making friends with others in the business will encourage them and give them free information and new ideas. When they hear the same things repeatedly, they will remember them effortlessly as the need arises. Encourage your down-line to attend regional and national conferences every time they have the chance to do so. Associating with other networkers in the industry will be beneficial for them, and they will pick up some tips on wealth creation, recruitment, advertising, free leads, and many other things that will help them within their business.

They will gain valuable information at a school or seminar and should make use of those opportunities often. Challenge the people in your group to take advantage of every opportunity that they have to attend a training event and you will see amazing things happening. You will all be making more money and living the lifestyles that you enjoy. Learn your business by heart, and your organization will grow because people will be asking how they can join your group when they see how successful it is.

## Becoming a leader

If you want to develop a successful network marketing business, the most important thing you can do is to learn how to be a leader.

Effective leaders will courageously accept responsibility and have the dedication to develop an atmosphere of enthusiasm and fulfilled dreams along a road to success that people will happily follow. Courageous, enthusiastic leaders think outside the box and are willing to do things in new ways. They attract success and encourage others to join them by showing them the awesome opportunities available in network marketing.

They know that they are accountable for teaching and supporting their teams as well as for giving them the tools to meet challenges that they may encounter. However, each team member is ultimately responsible for his/her own success or failure. Responsible leaders will teach and encourage their teams to be successful, but will not take over and do the work for them. Good leaders are dedicated to their business, to their people, and to success for each one. Leaders welcome the chance to help people change their lives for the better by assisting them to meet their goals and dreams.

Leaders establish an atmosphere of enthusiasm and excitement and the atmosphere they establish in their organizations determines whether they will grow, stand still, or die. Leaders who establish hopeful, enthusiastic atmospheres and demonstrate their dedication and helpfulness will attract the same type of people into their organizations.

People are attracted to leaders who show strength of character and charisma. People want to follow someone they feel they can trust to lead them to success. They want to join someone who makes them believe in themselves and believe that success is not only possible but also probable. Leaders teach their team members to expect to be successful and clearly outline each step of the process on the road to victory. They will teach their people not to choose to be successful, but to decide to be successful. They will encourage their down-line and praise them for small achievements and when their distributors are commended for small achievements, they will be encouraged to accomplish amazing triumphs.

To become an effective leader, you must first observe personal leadership habits yourself. If you want others to be courageous, dedicated, disciplined, and charismatic, you must lead them by your own example. Even if you are a born leader, you will gain valuable knowledge and develop and strengthen your leadership abilities through intensive study or with help from an experienced mentor.

There are many sources of help available, such as books, seminars, conference calls, and your own up-line. It will be worth the extra effort to become the best leader that you can be so that you can pass your knowledge on to your own business builders and develop an amazingly successful organization.

In the troubled economic times we are experiencing today, you would feel more financially secure if you did not have to depend on working for someone else to make a living. Layoffs and downsizing are all too common these days and it does not appear that things will improve any time soon. The answer for your wealth creation and financial stability could be network marketing.

You can be successful in multi-level marketing business even during your first year in the business. One of the secrets for success is to learn good communication skills. You may have made a list, joined one of the top companies in the industry with fabulous products and a great compensation plan, and you may have top help from your up-line, but if your communication skills are poor, your recruiting efforts will bring poor results.

You may be selling your MLM opportunity to people online with blogs, articles, or e-books. The internet is one of the best tools for building your business, but if you want to know how to have success with your home-based business, good communication is essential.

The telephone is another resource to use for prospecting when seeking people to join your business. You probably already have a phone service, so your telephone is a free recruitment tool. You can purchase some MLM leads and you can get some free leads. You can do cold calling and have an endless market, but you may have more success, especially in your first year, if you call people with whom you have some connection.

Call members of your church, your clubs, people you do business with, and people with whom you went to school. Learn how to present yourself and communicate so the people you call will respond to you. Learn to acquire a professional performer's personality and you should develop a great down-line for your home-based business. Maintain a positive, enthusiastic attitude even though many people will reject your opportunity.

When someone says no, do not let it get you down. Learn to laugh at rejection, and call the next one on your list. You may be uncomfortable calling people at first, but look your fears in the eye and keep going. When you believe in multi-level marketing, believe in yourself, are willing to make a commitment, and are willing to pay the price, you can become one of the best networkers in the industry.

## Starting a home-based business

A home-based network marketing business is one of the best ways to achieve long-term financial security.

A home-based network marketing business is one of the best ways to achieve long-term financial security. Your first year with a new company can be challenging, but with the right tools and tips, you can have success. It is important to have the right attitude. If you have the wrong idea about who you are, what commitment means, and how to develop good relationships, then working harder will not help because you will be working in the wrong way.

You may even have a positive attitude, but if you do not really believe that you can be successful, you won't be successful. You may know what you need to do, but knowing does not mean doing. Intending to do something doesn't mean that you will do it. People act according to how they think about life, themselves, commitment, loyalty, communication, and responsibility.

But even with all that information, many people don't do what it takes for wealth creation. Deciding to do something does not mean actually doing something. You can motivate people, but that motivation will not last unless you change the way they view things. You must have the right objectives and the right means to get the outcome that you desire. You can commit yourself to a goal even though you do not know how to achieve it. Your objective will produce the means necessary for success. When your objective is clear, the means will turn up. You don't need to know how to do things, but most people believe they must know how before they can reach their goal.

Ask a new prospect what his intention is for getting in the business. Ask yourself what your intention is when you share your opportunity. Search for ways to boost your intention and you are sure to find them.

If you want to build an awesome business, don't look for expertise or procedure; look at what is keeping you from really seeing the solutions.

Accept other points of view and when you start to see things differently, you will discover things that you could not see before. Those things were always there; you just didn't see them. You can't learn a new way to see things; you must experience changing your viewpoint for your-self; and when you do that, the possibilities are endless.

— Robert & Bonnie Butwin

# FROM ZERO TO MILLIONS STRATEGY

- Make people see things from a different perspective.
- Find your strong "why."
- FOCUS and COMMIT.
- Join the right company.
- Find a mentor.
- Develop habits of attitude.
- Set your goals.
- Your focus and dedication should go to your team.
- Remember the "Rule of Five."
- Training your down-line is crucial.
- Learn your business by heart.
- Associate with other networkers in the industry.
- Think outside the box as a leader.
- Dedicate yourself to your business, your people, and their success.
- Become an effective leader by developing personal leadership habits yourself.
- Become a skilled communicator.

# CHAPTER 9

# THE SPY THAT CAME IN OUT OF THE COLD

All right, Rod. Tell about yourself and your story. How did your network marketing career get started?

T he story is "The Spy That Came In Out of the Cold." The first $1 million I made was because I stepped on a landmine in Vietnam, got hospitalized in Japan, met a bunch of Japanese, got out of the army, came back to the U.S., went to college on a GI bill starving to death. There I discovered network marketing for Super Soap.

I then turned around and ended up going back to Japan and introducing the Super Soap there. So between June of 1969 and June of 1970, I made $386,000, which today is about $1.5 million. That was the first time.

The second time I hit $1 million was in a gasoline additive company. I'm a product guy. Money doesn't make much difference to me unless I go crazy over a product. I'm going to screw you if you don't buy it, but for your own good. That's because I believe in humanistic existentialism — you help people out whether they want it or not.

And as far as all the other stuff people have gone through, you've heard it all: liking people, staying in contact, making personal relationships, and everything. That's all pretty standard.

But what I did in 1974, I was in Amway, and I wrote my first training book. I'd got stuck in Amway for 18 months. Amway didn't want any part of it, so I got that training tool of a book, and I used to mail it to people. I had the thing about leadership on it, my picture on the cover with a big smile, and it bonded the people to me. They had this book in their hands with my picture and then I would get on training calls with them. Even though it was never really publicly published, that little training book did a lot of good for me.

What I tell people is that you have to make 50 to 100 phone calls a day, not 10 a day. That's too low and you will starve to death. You will never make a million dollars on that. Generally, my rate is 100 calls a day and most of them are 3-way calls. I teach my people to do 3-way calls with their warm market and I do the 3-way calls and just have them scheduled by the clock. Bam, bam, bam.

I checked today and one of my companies has had 2600 people sign up in the two weeks they've been open — 2600 people! That's on the main power leg and there are also other legs already coming in. How do you do that? You do it with new tactics and strategy for recession. You have to think out of the box, which right now means free sign up and free sample of the product. If somebody tries it, they think, "Wow!" This is why new out-of-the-box thinking is so important.

So you take internet automation combined with money. We have got to go out and raise several million dollars to give away all those samples, but one thing we know is that out of ten people that tried the sample, eight will buy it.

When I got involved with my next company, I was dead. Now, let me explain that. I had gone to Afghanistan and was whacked off; I was a spy. That's why I said you can name this chapter "The Spy That Came in Out of the Cold." The army "kills" you before you go. I was "killed" in a helicopter crash in Colorado and even my mother thought I was dead. I got my spine broken there. It's an hour-long story. That's why I said I'd keep it short. I fell and got my spine broken when I was there and was hospitalized. But, they were not going to let me out of the hospital and I said, "Why is that?" They said, "Because you're dead and we lost the paperwork." This is the army.

I went back to the ward and thought about it for a day and then I decided I'd had enough, so I walked down and said, "Goodbye!" And they said, "You can't leave, you're dead." And I said, "You cannot stop me from leaving because I'm dead."

So, I went back out to our home ranch in Colorado. My dad and I lasted two weeks together, then I went to my sister's in Denver and got picked up on this hot new product in Mexico, which was great stuff. It was a fantastic fuel modifier. It would take an old wreck and turn it into a hot rod, just to make it short. Miracle product! I loved it because I was product-driven.

I told you — I am a product guy. Off I went with that and built it up and ended up living in Southern California before, finally, at the end of that year the army brought me back alive and demanded that I show up or they were going to send people after me to handcuff and court marshal me.

The company got shut down as well. The stuff we were selling, which was Methyl Tertiary Butyl Ether, MTBE, was great for cutting down emissions, but they found out it could harm the groundwater. So all of a sudden, they outlawed MTBE as a gasoline additive. Understand that when they put it in gasoline for emissions, they took a little pint bottle and put it in a 10,000 gallon tank of gasoline. One little bottle. We would take a bottle of it and put the whole thing into a 20-gallon gas tank, and it would just "boom"! And it was like putting a supercharger on a car. So ,that one was worth a million bucks and that was what I collected that year that I was "dead."

My next experience was with Slick 50®, an engine additive, and it took a lot longer. You'll see it in U.S. auto parts stores today. It is in a black box. I took that to the market and hit that hard and was making $1.2 million a year when they shut it down.

This was all while I was still in the army. At that time, the army got the first 10 hours. I gave MLM the second 10 hours and then the other four hours I started the *Golden Opportunity Magazine*. It was the first print mail magazine in America Web Press. It was for advertising that generated leads for Slick 50®. And I put it down on a magazine of about 24 pages. It worked pretty well.

Two friends of mine came along from "Forever Living" and said, "Rod, could we do that? Would you do that magazine for us if you could? And could you take those ugly Slick 50® pictures off and put in our 'Aware and Forever Living' ones?" And I said, "Yeah, but I need about 5,000 people, because that's what I've got." I didn't want to rip people off, so I didn't make it a high profit margin. But I just pinched that 10% and then ran it on a 10% margin of what I made, which was 10%. And they signed up and six months later, I had 60,000 distributors.

I'm in the army, doing Slick 50®. But I got some good people running and I was still primarily writing for the magazine and writing the stuff about MLM. And, of course, it was helping build my Slick 50®, which was in the late 80's. Then in 1992, Slick 50® killed off the distributors and went into just straight retail and I sued them and collected $10 million, giving half of it to my downline.

I had one friend that committed suicide. He had cancer. So I took care of his family, his kids, college, paid for their house and everything and had about $5 million left, but it was less than that after taxes.

So right now, primarily, what I do is help start out new MLM companies. Generally, if you see a billion-dollar MLM company, I had my fingers in it. I'm considered one of the best comp plan experts and consultants in the industry. And the other thing I do is mergers and acquisitions, buying and selling MLM companies.

I've got $20 to $40 million right now, sitting in a pot, waiting to buy companies here that look to be a big deal. So my goal right now is to make a million a year in MLM doing mergers and acquisitions. I don't think that I am going to make it this year, but next year I will.

## With 20/20 hindsight

If I were to do it all over again, I would have published the training book I did in 1974 publicly. I would have gone ahead and published it and put it on the marketplace, because it wouldn't go out there like a generic book. It gathered more fame and fortune, but I kind of kept it as my own secret weapon. If I had gone ahead and published that in 1974, that would have been a huge advantage. But you have to remember that back then, book distribution was a lot harder, too. There weren't any newspapers, there weren't any magazines.

Most new distributers are told to call 100 people they know in order to start the business. I tried to make those 3-way calls. In the book, I trained people on 3-way calls, how to do them, how to time them, how to schedule them and everything. If I could get a schedule going doing 3-way calls with a person, that was a plus.

One of the things I teach is this: "Don't try to argue anybody into it. If they're not interested, move on."

It's like the pearl thing. A lot of people in MLM do this. If they don't find a pearl, they close the oyster up, stick it under their armpit, and limp around looking for a pearl. And the way you find pearls is shucking more oysters. The more oysters you shuck, the more pearls you will have a chance to find.

## Using the internet to accelerate your business

Well, to accelerate the internet, you go out and set up good landing pages. I mean, there's 20 different ways. I went over people's head this afternoon when I offered to give them a free book that they could put up and use as an internet site to collect leads, to generate leads.

And I've got more than a hundred websites out there that are on lead generation or in The MLM Watchdog, which has been on the front page of Google. If you search for MLM in Google, the MLM Watchdog has been on the front page, somewhere between number one and number seven, ever since Google was born. Of course, there's a lot of stuff on it, and thousands of people linked to it. You have people looking for information. It's a big website, the MLM Watchdog. I'm going to guess I'm almost about to break a thousand pages. A lot of it is archived or history. But some of those archived pages are several pages back.

I look for links. One of the things I did, I put on the Watchdog page and I don't have anything to do with it. It's a client of mine. But, I put it on there: "Free Sign Up For Free Product" for that thing where we're running recession-time offers. I threw that on the Watchdog, which I do for just about any company if it's a brand new company.

## The right mindset

I'm a military guy. I'm fighting a war and I'm going to win. Period. Zip. Zero. Military guys don't go out and train to lose wars. You train to win wars. I just accept everyone and look at every one of them as war.

I started in the military in 1964. And I just got out of there for a while to go to college and get a degree and get a commission as an author. Then I went back in the army. That's when I started doing MLM, when I was out of the army. I came back into the army and they said, "Okay, you're an officer now. You can't bartend. You can't drive taxi cabs. You can't sell life insurance." I said, "What about MLM?" It was the only thing they didn't say no to.

To improve myself, I studied. There were some tapes around but not too many. They were just trying anything back through the 70's and the 80's and there wasn't a lot of anything published on MLM.

For the new network marketer, I would say, number one is to read *Big Al Tells All* by Tom Big Al Schreiter. Period. Because Tom takes it from the simplest stuff.

Another one is *Mary Kay, on People Management*. That's a little more for the corporate side, but there's a wealth of news in there. And to prove it, the book is about 20 years old now and the price of it is about $12 or $13 on Amazon. I think that will pretty well cover it, because Tom gives good basic information. I'd also say Jim Rohn. He has the best CD on your first year in network marketing.

## Lead generation

The one thing everybody skips is a warm list. But if you don't hit it, and people are still hungering, you've got to have a good, honest source of leads. And those are hard to come by. They are very hard to come by.

I used to own a publishing house auction where they'd come in and sell remnant leads, so to speak, for a weight loss business opportunity. But it got so dirty that I shut it down. And I have a hard time now going on to buy any leads. So, if I were going to go back full time to do a million dollar run based on building an MLM alone, I'd have to throw up another hundred websites or so to get enough quality leads.

Because what you do when you're doing quality leads, you pre-expose them. You take them to a landing page that has a quick glimpse about the product and about the opportunity. And then it sorts them out. Are they interested, click here and get a free something: a free e-book or free "How to Make a Million Bucks." So, what kind of e-Book would pull right now, today? Maybe "How to Save $100 a Week Out of Your Budget," or "How to Make Cold Cash Quick," or something like that. You've got to have something to pull them in to form a relationship.

I've sat here and heard people say, "I have formed a relationship," whether they are in MLM or not. Well, how do you form a relationship? You give people cookies first, right? Something that tastes good. And the cheapest way to do it is by e-books or special reports. It works that way, all the way back when we used to do magazine advertising.

— Rod Cook

## FROM ZERO TO MILLIONS STRATEGY

· Read the book *Big Al Tells All* by Tom Big Al Schreiter.
· Create landing pages for generating leads: free e-books, reports, etc.
· Develop new tactics and strategies to beat the recession by thinking "outside the box."

# CHAPTER 10

# FROM BAD COP TO EDUCATOR

Hello, Ken, tell about how you started in network marketing?

W ell, in spite of me earning $100,000 per year in each of the previous 10 years in police work, I was dead broke. My spending habits were going out faster than what was coming in and had finally caught up with me. With a mortgage, car payments, and over $250,000 in credit card debt, I decided to take action and I found network marketing.

I fell in love with it because it was such an easy concept to understand. In my first year, I got my group to 3,000 people and I was making $25,000 per month. And then, in my twelfth month, it completely collapsed — because of me. I was a dictator.

Because I had been a cop since I was 18 years old, the only way I knew how to lead was by force, telling people what to do. And I was really,

really hard on people. If people didn't recruit others, I would make fun of them. I would be very rude to them in front of others, telling them they should quit because they suck and all these other things. It was bad!

And then one day my two top leaders quit and 90% of my group fell apart. My income went from 25 grand to 3 grand in one month. So, I decided to write a book about my experience. It's called *From Here to Having It All*. Basically, I realized that there are really only two things you need to do to make money in this business and they're the same in every business. It's really that simple.

The first thing you have to learn are business-specific leadership skills to lead this sort of organization into space. This is very challenging, because everybody's a volunteer. But you still have to learn to lead them. It's like leading any volunteer organization to all their effective partners.

And then, the second thing is you have to learn lead generation. You have to teach people to generate leads and show them how to work in their warm market and turn cold markets into warm markets. You have to provide them with options for generating leads.

If you can master those two simple things, you can make millions and millions of dollars in this business. And it's not difficult. But it takes s specific set of skills and your skills in this business are very closely tied to your personality. It's a business of loving people and you just have to remember that.

## Learning from experiences

When my group fell apart, I went out and started trying to find the right way to lead. And luckily for me, at that very time, there was a guy that I had sponsored in Vancouver who didn't know what had happened with most of the group. He had sponsored a guy in Mexico, who was a Canadian expatriate living in Mexico. He used to call me all the time and was bugging me to fly down to Mexico and help him talk to some people and get his business going.

Because my group in Canada had just fallen apart, I said, "Sure. Why not? I'll go down to Mexico." And it was a really difficult time for me. I was very lost. I was trying to figure out how you only have one personality. And, the hardest thing to do is to recognize the flaws in your own personality.

But I had to change because my group was falling apart. Obviously, there was an issue. So I was trying to find out the right way to be. I was in Mexico and talking to this guy's friends and that's when I met Juan Carlos.

It was on the last day and he had asked me to meet this guy and his wife who've been these big leaders in the Amway business. And I literally met with them for three hours because I was trying to find the right way to be.

I met him and it was an amazing experience because he's a great person. He loves people. Everybody loves him. So I ride in and I started calling him every day, taking notes. I would ask him, "How do you deal with people like this? How did you learn to love people? What's your background?" Just like you are doing now with these interviews!

I was learning. All of sudden, I started to grow and realized that I could love people and, in fact, anybody can. Then, out of the blue, he says, "Okay. I'm going to join your business." And that's when I learned that lesson that you have to get people to like you and trust you. And the fastest way to do it is to really, honestly want to be friends with people and form those relationships. And Juan Carlos has been teaching me ever since.

In fact, he joined my network? And we kept working and building the business. Back in last January, I was terminated from the company that I was working for. Ten months ago, I was making $150,000 a month. And that's something that I learned the hard way in network marketing. Unless you set the relationship up properly in the company in the beginning, you don't own your business.

I do own my company because I have a contract that suffered from the policies and procedures that is very, very detailed on how it's set up. But average people don't own their businesses.

I was terminated because my reputation was growing faster than the company's. And I was selling the book that I wrote, which I had written because a lot of people had encouraged me to when my dad died of Lou Gehrig's disease at the age of 54. I wrote the book and donated all the royalties to ALS research.

So the CEO of that company started to tell me not to speak in public anymore, not to go to major events, not to speak at the Mastermind Event and all these things. And when I refused, he just terminated me. It has really taught me some interesting dynamics about business, because they started a whole smear campaign after that. They caused a big lawsuit with other network marketing companies. The CEO of the company lied under oath and in court documents and perjured themselves and, basically, said it was all my fault. But, despite that, it's been a really great learning experience.

## Getting it right the next time around

Right from the onset, we went out and looked at 120 different companies to choose the one that we're in now. You need to have a consumable product that's unique, that is totally different than anything else that's out there — preferably nutraceutical supplements of some sort that have science to back them up.

You need to be in a company that's young enough that nobody knows about it, because in America, that's important. But it should also have the ability and the desire to go internationally fast. And we also wanted to be in a company that was funded properly and that had a lot of money. Because the last company I was in, they're broke. They had no money and they kept lying to people about it.

When we got set up with them, we created a contract that the owners had to agree that we build the business. I'd go out and sell books and tapes that are going to bring the company a lot of business. And also, the company doesn't own my down-line. If they're going to take disciplinary action against any of our people, then they have to talk to me first. And we have to talk through it at work. They have to sign off on all of those types of things. So it's a new format. It's unusual.

Yeah. We do a lot of things in our network that are really different. We own a lead generation company online. So we have an affiliate marketing such as CarbonCopyPro, MLM Lead System Pro, and these types of businesses. So, basically, when somebody joins our team, they actually join an organization called "EvolvLife Team." Our company's website is www.evolvhealth.com. In there is a back office. Every one of our people joins two things; they join our company and they join our team. We produce all of our books and training materials, CD' s, and DVD' s.

All the money that we make goes into a profit-sharing model like a transparent bank account. It's kind of like a public company in our back office. All the profits, every month, go into one account. And we pay it equally to every member of the community, based on their pin level, how many people are in their down-line, and how much money their people are spending in our system. We developed a software system built for that.

So, you make your full-time income from the company and you make your full-time income from the team. And we've created it so it's the same amount. So, if you're making $20,000 a month from the company, you're also making $20,000 a month from the team. It doubles the amount of money you can make.

In terms of duplication, you have to be innovative. There's only one way to do the business, at the core of the business. You've got to keep constantly recruiting people; you have to have a getting-started methodology that is consistent through the entire organization that understands that theory that the most important minute is the minute they say, "Yes!" And then, as you go beyond the minutes after they join, it's a sliding scale.

You've got to get them started as fast as possible. You get them going up that ladder of belief or they will go down. And so we have a methodology for that which is identical throughout our entire organization. That's what's duplicated. And that core methodology has to be the same. We've just created a model where the only way people can participate in that profit-sharing model in the team is if they are using the methodology. So, it's like paying people to be duplicable. It's just an added incentive.

What's more, every leader has to be a follower. That's what it comes down to. Very important. In fact, I think leadership is a decision to follow. That's been a good definition of leadership — a conscious decision to follow.

## Increasing your success

If I look at the last several years, the most important thing is that people join YOU. They're not joining the business. And I have to constantly work on being the best me I can be. Literally, I am looking in the mirror and deciding, first of all, what does the best ME look like? I have to realize that people are going to follow me. They're going to want to join the business with me. So I have to be — body, mind and spirit — constantly in the best shape I can be.

And I'm not in the best shape right now. So I'm working out. I'm trying to eat right and be healthy. Right down to severely limiting my alcohol consumption. Everything I do every single day, I have to be cognizant of how other people perceive me. And that's hard to do.

One of the things Art Jonak taught me, and I love this, is the idea that being a leader means that you give up your rights because you're under a microscope. And you have to work on being the right example all the time. And that's just the incredibly important part. How badly you want it will determine how badly you pursue it.

And also, for me, I'd never ever stop. You wouldn't even know the person I was seven years ago. If we sat side by side, we'd probably be totally different people. How I dress, how I act — it's completely, radically different. And that's by design.

And I read at least an hour a day now and listen to at least an hour of audio leadership CDs a day. I've read over 300 books on leadership and personal development in the last five years. I'm constantly reading three books at the same time. And I've always spent at least 15 minutes a day in prayer. I'm a big believer. It doesn't matter what faith you are, but everybody needs to have faith of some sort. So that's definitely one.

The other thing that I think would be key, that's part of leadership, too, is that the speed of the team will only ever be half the speed of the leader. That's part of number one, too — setting the right example.

The second thing would be recruiting. The reason I recruit so many people and talk to so many people is because I want to set the right example. I don't ever expect anybody to do it at the level I do it, but I do 20 contacts every day knowing that my group will do two or three. If I'm only talking to three or four people a day, then my group will do zero. It's all about setting the right example.

I never stop recruiting people. And Jordan does 20 a day, too. He just doesn't look at it the same way. If he's recruiting two or three people a month, sponsoring them, you have to interact with dozens of people a day, building relationships.

It's just talking to people. It's a people business. Mark Yarnell wrote a book called *Your First Year In Network Marketing*. That's a very important book to read if you're putting this together and you want it to be really perceived as added value for people. One of his most famous quotes is, "The lifeblood of the business is the new blood." So it's all about new people. Momentum is your ability to out-pace attrition, right? You're always going to have attrition. You can't control it.

The two types of mindset in network marketing are those that lagged the dog and those that really deeply understand the business and understand that creating the right culture and the right team will keep the most people motivated for the longest time. But the most you can do is to create the right family. Then it's a matter of creating a culture where there's so many people coming in that it gets exciting and more people will stay around because they want to be part of that. So, it's really important to create a culture where people are constantly recruiting and being rewarded for recruiting, even for the little steps of just sponsoring one person. And then the third is the community.

Everybody wants to be a part of something. There's a hierarchy of needs. Most people have heard of Abraham Maslow. Maslow's hierarchy is seven levels. You can really simplify that to basically three levels. The first is a need for financial security. Jordan Adler actually proved this point this morning at the meeting. The first is financial security; the second is respect; and the third is legacy. And everybody wants to be a part of that. Once you've got all the money, then you've got the friendships. I'm thinking of being a part of something, giving back, that's legacy.

So I have to build a community that people want to be a part of that has a mission and a statement. So you'll see on our website that our mission statement is to create a global community of millions of tomorrow's leaders. That's our mission statement. Everybody in the team knows that they're a part of that. That's not Ken Dunn's mission statement. That's everybody buying into it because they want to be a part of that.

And so, I'm creating an environment where people can come in and feel comfortable enough to grow because in order for people to grow, they have to be truly willing to confront the worst side of them. You must be able to create an environment where people feel comfortable looking at their flaws through love and respect and trust and truth. Then once they're in that community, you have to focus everybody on becoming a better leader and take their minds off how much money they can make, but instead creating the culture where everybody's focused on becoming a better person.

When you say to become a better leader, that confuses people. What we actually teach in our team is being better parents, better siblings, better members of our community, and being better spouses. And when we have our leadership events in our company, in our team, we don't even talk about our company or our product. It's just about leadership.

So that's the third thing. It's building a community that people want to be a part of. It's the tie that binds everybody together.

And you can see how it works because if you build a community, people will come into it that are willing to grow. And when they're willing to grow, they'll find it easier to bring in more people. And when they start introducing people to come into the community, for its benefit here, then it all works together. And through osmosis, they end up making more money. But they're not solely focused on making money.

## Lead generation

First of all, one of the theories I have in my book that so many people struggle so much in lead generation and recruiting is they don't look at recruiting the right way. Recruiting is a two-part process. And everybody thinks it's one. The first part I call procurement. And the second part is processing. What does the word "procure" mean? It means to get, to gather, to collect, right? That's the lead generation. That's the procurement part. And then the processing is what you do with those leads when you get them.

But only one of those two things is duplicable. So the procurement side has to fit your personality. The processing side, that's three steps — introduce them to your website, your opportunity. Give them the chance to evaluate or follow-up. Call them. Refer them and follow-up. Use the sales funnel. That's creativity. That could be whatever your prescription is in the team. But the procurement side has to fit the way somebody is. So in our team, we present our people. First they have to go through their list.

We have that process we use so that everybody gets started the right way: by doing a home meeting, meeting with their top five people, and meeting with their sponsor. But then after they get through their list, nobody is ever going to make a million dollars in network marketing with the people they know.

So then, we have to teach our people procurement methodologies. And there are not a lot of teams that understand this. There are not a lot of people that do it. But we have a core list of 14 different ways to procure leads that we teach our people. We expose them to each one, ask them to try them out, then see which they like the best. It's everything from going up to strangers, to putting signs on the back of your car, to running newspaper ads, to our internet methodology.

We have an online affiliate marketing company with a $39.95 per month fee. Basically, it teaches you how to create a sales funnel. And it's very, very dynamic how it works. So at first, it's called "branding yourself." We teach people how to brand themselves properly.

Do we tell new people to call their 100 friends and family? We did that in the beginning, because that's where they're going to have the easiest time recruiting people. But that's just the beginning. We want our people to stay with us their entire lives, so we've got to keep feeding them and helping them to grow that way.

One of the things we do with everybody is we have a back office in our team that every member of our community signs up for, which is the online lead generation. We teach them to have a landing page that's just a video message with an opt-in for a new web account that gets their name and their phone number. When they opt in, they go into another auto responder, but they get forwarded to a second page, a "thank you" page, which you can customize. So it's a video from you plus a bit more information, then they get to an application where they can click to acquire and ask all the standard questions: why do you want a part time job? What's your life right now? How much money do you make now? How much time can you commit? When can you get started? And then, when they hit "enter," that application gets sent to you and they get forwarded to a business page where it explains all about our opportunity. But they've already gone through two different steps.

Now you know they're really serious about it. And then the back office also has all of the scripts so that they can call the prospect back with the answer to the questions and say, "Okay, this is what you said here. Here is what it means, etc." and build rapport. It's all part of the system and every one of our members has access to it.

Even if they're not building online, they can, on their business cards, have the URL for their personal website and use the sales funnel that's created.

Another thing we do on a weekly basis is have online webinars and calls where we teach people how to use social media like Facebook, Twitter, and YouTube and how to use pass-by ads to generate leads. They send the leads to the landing page that capture the information and process them, for free!

That's how serious we are about this! It'll be at 100,000 within the next 24 months, easily. Within 24 months from now, I'll have three or four people who will become seven-figure earners.

Juan Carlos will be one of those seven-figure earners for sure. I will be, obviously, and another guy, Mike Hugley, who's been with me for five months. He's already had weeks as big as $10,000.

It's working in your local market; going through your warm market first, then creating a methodology to get started properly yourself. You get started and stay started. That's the secret!

Even the way that I act — very loud, very fast, very excited — that's by design. It gets more people fired up. I could slow myself down and be just like Jordan in front of a room. But I found that the results get more exciting when you stay fired up. At least that's what I think works best for me.

## Having mentors

I've had many mentors in different areas of my life for different things. Art Jonak, he's the same age as me. I'm building more aggressively than he is right now, but he's a much better leader than I am and I look at him as my mentor. I have mentors in my mortgage business. Everything I've done in my life. Whenever I've decided I wanted to do something, I go find somebody who's the best at it.

In network marketing, Art Jonak has been a big influence on me. Orjan Saele, Art's best friend, is another mentor of mine. Juan Carlos Barrios has been a great mentor for me as well. Those three, basically, have been the most influential to me.

Juan Carlos has taught me how to love people. He also taught me the importance of training tools and systems. That's a very important part. Art Jonak has really, really helped me to understand the power of the profession! But from a personal perspective, he's really been the best example of a leader for me personally and helped me understand about sacrificing in your life if you truly have that desire to be a leader. I've never actually told him this, but Art Jonak is probably the best example of leadership for me. And, I don't follow what people tell me to do; I follow what I see in people. And that's a conscious decision that I've made.

You follow what they do and not necessarily what they say because actions speak louder than words. You want people to "walk the walk and talk the talk."

I wrote a book about mentorship because there are so many things to learn. Mentorship is a two-way street and any type of properly set up mentorship relationship needs to be win-win. There needs to be something in it for the mentor as well. Art Jonak's example has been so valuable to me; that's why I'm so involved in what he does for this profession.

I've made some adjustments in my business style because of him trusting me enough to be part of this. He asks me to speak every year at his event, and I bring my people to his events. I mastermind because of that. It's my way to help him in the same way he's helped me. And that's a really important part of respecting a mentor, of having mentors in your life.

## Masterminds

In our community, we have what we call our leadership council. It's a team of our top seven people. I don't make any decisions singly for the organization even though it's my down-line. It's much bigger than that and if people believe that, we nullify the fact that it truly isn't collective. The mastermind group in your organization should always be your top performers, because the top leaders are the ones that are leading most groups. You can never get a group of people to work together unless they truly believe that their importance is valued and that they have been the latitude to lead their organizations, which are part of your organization.

It's like Jordan said, "I've got seven big teams." He didn't say, "I have a big team." He said "I have seven leaders that I've sponsored who have large organizations." And they are responsible for 93% of his income. All of my checks come from four people right now. I'm up to 60 thousand a month again, already, in seven months.

## Habits to live by

My number one priority is my God, my second priority is my family, and my third is my business. And I live by that. I start everyday at 6:30 a.m. in the morning. I wake up and pray and then I get on an exercise bike, a recumbent bike, where I ride for an hour. It's hard while I'm riding in an aerobic state and can't even talk, but I read. I've ruined so many books by sweating on them. But I still read the entire time that I'm riding. I have to multitask — it's just the way I am hardwired.

I take care of my body, mind, and spirit at the same time. And whenever I travel and stay at different hotels, I ask them at the concierge,

"Do you have a functioning recumbent bike in your gym?" And if they don't, I won't stay there, because I'm just that methodical.

So after the hour on the bike reading, I read the Bible for 15 minutes a day, read the scriptures. Then I have breakfast after that. I have a very strict schedule of my day, everyday. We do a call at 9:00 a.m. every morning. Even at sea here, I've been on the call every day with my entire community. It's a leadership call.

I have the call at 9:00 a.m. EST every morning for 15 minutes for the entire team. Right now, we're averaging about 400 people a day and it will get into the thousands. We have one devotional tip, one leadership tip, and one business-building tip that we deliver everyday throughout our organization. And that's extremely important, to get everybody in the team focused in the same direction: learning leadership.

After that call, I spend a half hour checking emails, Facebook, Twitter, social media, and adjusting my lead capture pages and all that. From about 10:30 a.m. until noon, I'm prospecting. I have to get my 20 people a day. And then I'll have lunch, sometimes a lunch meeting, sometimes with my family if I'm anywhere near home.

Then in the afternoon, I'll spend a couple of hours working with the team, then some more time prospecting from 3:00 — 5:00 p.m. Family time is from 5:00 — 7:00 p.m. and then I am back to working the business from 7:00 — 9:00 p.m., Monday to Thursday. Friday nights I take off. On Saturdays, I do trainings. I take Sundays off. Every week is like that and it will be like that until I'm making $100,000 a month.

Basically, the methodology is that until you're making $10,000, 90% of your time needs to be prospecting; from $10,000 to about $30,000, it's 70% of your time; from $30,000 to $50,000, it's 50% of your time; and then $50,000 to a $100,000, it's 30% of your time. It depends on whatever your time commitment is.

As soon as I get to $100,000 a month, I'll slow down a lot. I'll spend more time reading. As my income gets higher, I'll go from an hour reading a day to an hour and a half a day to two hours a day. When I'm at a hundred grand again, I'll be reading around two or three hours per day, just constantly working on being the best leader that I can be.

The higher your income becomes, the more you spend time improving yourself. Why? Because, first of all, it keeps you sharp. The head swells with the pocket book. It just does. And then you also have more responsibility to lead. So you need to be constantly sharpening the axe. And that's a great analogy.

I need to be talking again about edification, which is a very important subject. I've made some really bad mistakes not edifying people that were struggling to make money. Then they left the group. They never worked out. And it makes the whole community dysfunctional. You need to edify and be a true leader to those people in your organization.

— Ken Dunn

## FROM ZERO TO MILLIONS STRATEGY

· Learn business-specific leadership skills.
· Learn lead generation, how to work in your warm market and how to turn cold markets into warm market.
· Contract with your company and set up a proper agreement so you own your business.
· Find a company that has a lot of money.
· In theory, the most important minute is the minute you sponsor someone and get them started as fast as possible.
· Every leader has to be a follower.
· People join YOU, not just your company.
· Setting the right example is being the right example to other people.
· Learn recruiting.
· Momentum is your ability to out-pace attrition.
· Create a culture where people are constantly recruiting and being rewarded for recruiting.
· Create a community.
· Learn the methodology for income vs. time:
    — Until you're making $10,000, 90% of your time needs to be prospecting.
    — From $10,000 to about $30,000, it's 70% of your time.
    — From $30,000 to $50,000, it's 50% of your time.
    — And then $50,000 to a $100,000, it's 30% of your time.

## CHAPTER 11

# LIVING UP TO YOUR LEGACY

Alright, Travis and Summer, tell me a little bit about your journey in the network marketing business. How did you start and what is your story?

———

Seven years ago, we were in the mortgage industry. And life was good in the mortgage industry at that time. We had a very substantial six-figure income and we had grown accustomed to that income. But we woke up one morning to an email that the company that we had worked for was closing down. It was a big shock for us. But we're both optimists and thought, "Hey, no big deal. We'll go out and get another job."

And so I started interviewing with other companies and as quickly as we would interview with those companies, they were also closing down. It was kind of the tip of the iceberg, the start of the demise of the mortgage industry. And, of course, Summer was a full-time stay-at-home mother. We had three children that were three years of age or under at the time, all in diapers. So it was a little bit stressful.

Month one came and went, still no job, but we were still pretty optimistic. Month two came and went. Month three came and went. And by the fourth month, things started to get pretty interesting for us. We started selling off all our toys and there were lots of garage sales. It got pretty difficult.

In fact, I remember distinctly at one point having our electricity and gas turned off. We had a tow truck driver repossess one of our vehicles, and another tow truck driver looking for our other vehicle. At one point, we had to take our children upstairs and hide them in the bedroom. We had the tow truck driver at our front door and we didn't want them to know we were home because we didn't want to lose the last vehicle we had. So that's where we were at.

It led Summer and me to sit down and have a conversation about what we were going to do. And it's interesting, if you take a look at most people today, most people don't have a clear definition of what they want their financial freedom to look like.

## Financial freedom

Your financial freedom is the day that you no longer have to trade time for dollars. You can do the things that you want to do as opposed to the things that you have to do.

We would wake up in the morning, grab our car keys and just start driving, not knowing where we were headed. But that's how we live our lives, right?

Summer: And I think that we had been kind of living our lives like that up until that point because we didn't really think about where we wanted our destination to be. We were doing well. We just lived day to day doing the same thing over and over again, but without really having a goal. We didn't have any growth pattern or growth in our journey.

We decided to sit down on a Sunday night at the kitchen table, stack of bills this high and just start talking about what our dream life looked like. We thought that if we started at the end, maybe a road map would appear or something.

So, we started talking about what that dream life would look like for us. It was interesting because we talked about the materialistic things like nicer cars and a nicer home, but, ultimately, the conversation turned to the things that were a little bit more meaningful. In fact, we started talking about the most important thing to us, which was our time.

## Time can never come back

Your time is the most valuable commodity that you have. And you'll never get your time back. This led us into a discussion about residual income. We didn't know what a residual income was. We never had a residual income. But, we just knew that if we were ever going to get the time to be able to do what we wanted to do, we had to go out and acquire some type of asset that was going to produce money that would pay us month after month. So we started looking at a lot of different industries.

Summer: We quickly found the jobs that were available or the things that we were looking at didn't fit our goals. And it became kind of frustrating at certain points because we were like, "What do we do? We know we need to have money. We need to support our family. But these things don't feel right. That's not what we want. Do we just do these anyway for now?" It was actually quite a dilemma because we were in a situation where we had to produce something now for survival. But we didn't want to just settle, because we had finally decided what we wanted. And I think that was a monumental time for us to make that choice.

We had to choose with that mindset. We knew what we wanted, but when it came down to that decision, would we have what it takes to just make that choice?

We have spoken earlier about having to make that choice. And once you make that choice, you don't even look in that direction anymore. You just keep going. But you have to have that goal. You have to find what you want first.

So we needed a vehicle. We started looking, first at franchises. They were a little bit too expensive. We didn't have any money. We looked at the real estate market. At that point, our 500 FICO score wasn't going to take us very far because our credit was suffering.

And then I had a friend that was calling. He had been calling over the past few months, telling me that he had an opportunity that he wanted to share with me. And up to that point, I had a lot of preconceived notions about any opportunities when people call. But I was at a point where I was extremely humble. I was starting to realize that the height of all stupidity is forming an opinion without knowing all the facts. I decided to take the meeting.

We ended up golfing. I thought, at the very least, I'll get 18-holes out of it. On the first hole, I'll never forget it, he turned around and he said to me, "I've got this direct sales opportunity that I want to share with you. I don't know much about the industry. But what I do know is you can position yourself in the beginning stages with the company that has all of the signs of really being one of the next big hitters in the industry. And you go to work and you work hard over the next one or two years; there's a lot of money that can be made."

It sounded pretty good to me. We were in a position where we didn't have anything to lose and it was a minimal cost to get started. So, over the next two years, we failed miserably.

Summer: Actually, we were so tight with money at that time. I think we had to borrow some of the money from friends and family. It was embarrassing. But I'm really proud of that journey and that story. I mean, it is what it is. If there's a will, there's a way and we were one of those people.

We were really, really tight with money at that time. We wanted to do it, but we were like, "How do we do this?" When there's a will, there's a way. We had made that choice and we knew what we wanted to do. We had set our goals, there was no turning back, and we found a way. It's interesting, because you do come in contact with people who are in that same position. And now I can say, very truthfully, "I understand what you're going through." But you have to make that choice and have that commitment. And you have to do whatever it takes.

So, we failed miserably the first two years. At the end of two years, Summer sat me down, like wives do sometimes and basically said, "You've got a couple of options. Option number one is you can go out and get a real job. Or option number two is you can figure out how to make this work. But we've borrowed as much money as we could from our friends and family at this point."

I subscribe to a philosophy in life that if you truly want to be successful in any area, find yourself a thoroughbred and just try to keep up. I believe heavily in the concept of coaching and mentorship. So I set out to find a coach and a mentor. And I found somebody who was living in Provo with whom we aligned ourselves, which was one of the top producers — not just in the country, but in the world. He sort of took us under his wing over the next year.

This man taught me three things about this industry that have really changed our path, our journey. I was out there selling and telling and trying to convince people to join our business. My product is better than your product. My company is better than your company. And we were out there selling and telling like the best of them, but they call this network marketing for a reason, not network sales. And anytime that you're out there selling and you're trying to convince, you're not going to get the results that you're looking for. People put up a wall on a subconscious level. And so he taught me three things.

He taught me, number one, that this business is about growing yourself as a leader, because people naturally gravitate towards leadership. He taught me, number two, that this business is about helping people go from where they are today to where it is that they want to be, which hinges on number one. And number three, it's about relationships, just establishing relationships and nurturing those relationships. So, we stopped selling, we stopped telling. We stopped trying to convince people to join our business. And we started focusing on what we had to offer from a leadership standpoint, from a systematic standpoint and even from a personal standpoint.

And an interesting thing happened. People started to come to us because of what we had to offer. Our organization first started to grow across the state and then slowly across the country. Then we woke up one day with people in Japan in our organization. That was a pretty fun day because that's the point we realized who we were literally making money 24 hours a day, seven days a week. And that's a fun, exciting time.

So for us, over the past three or four years now, when we look at that fulcrum point, or that key moment that really allowed us to start having success, it was that commitment to personal growth — growing ourselves as leaders, getting our hands on any type of reading material, aligning ourselves with individuals that can contribute to us and add value to who we are. We've had a lot of mentors along the way.

What we've created is an organization that focuses and hones in on that personal development. It's called Legacy. And it's focused around a concept called the "Law of Legacy" that John C. Maxwell teaches. And that's what we do now. It's not about bringing people in the door. That's what people don't understand about this industry. It's about keeping them in and moving them along and letting them grow. It's about developing leaders rather than maintaining followers. And that's what most people don't understand.

Summer: There are a few people who operate that way. But in actuality, when leaders emerge, they don't allow them to really fully develop as leaders. They still want to keep them captive under their leadership. I think that when we say it, we have to mean it. And you have to allow others to grow in their journey, whatever that looks like for them. Make that decision for them and then help them get to that journey without any limitations on them.

And, you know, a lot of leaders out there really want their followers. But I believe that the number one way to grow in an organization is to grow the people in the organization. And that also means that you have to keep growing. Because if you stop growing, that's when they'll supersede where you are.

In our journey, it's been interesting to see where we're at today. We come to a trip like this and realize, when you surround yourself with the Art Jonaks and the Jordan Alders of the world, that there's so much growth to go. And that's exciting for us.

We look back seven years ago to that moment, then to where we are today, knowing that we've got a thriving business and we're getting ready to publish our first book, which is coming out in February. It's not about network marketing. It's more about the 17 Laws of Living Your Legacy.

It's fun to think about how far we've come, but we also know how far we still have to go. It's a fun place to be right now. So, this trip is, for us, kind of monumental, as far as what network marketing can do for you, and just how far we've come.

## Your mindset

Summer: I really think it comes down to really believing in yourself and believing in your "why," whatever your reasons are. That's why it is so important to sit down and figure out what you want, not just personally, but as a couple, if you are married. Figure out what you want for your family, and really believe in that. People don't really look at that, at the beginning, and understand their "why." I think it is easy for them to forget and just go back into the system that we all have been programmed with. Know what you want and know where you're going. I think that when you don't, that's when you tend to lose sight of things. That's what I believe.

I have hung onto a story that I heard in my first year in network marketing. It was told by a gentleman who had been very successful in the corporate side. In fact, he'd been one of the founders of one of the largest network marketing companies out there. When he sold that company, he decided to go to work as a distributor. And he thought that because he was who he was, he would just show up and rooms would be full.

So he joined this company and he decided to go travel the road. He was going to spend about a year on the road building. He advertised before he went into the cities. He showed up in the first city and there was only one person in the room. And it was just him and his cousin. So, it wasn't a great meeting.

They went on to the next city and, again, nobody's there. They continued to do this for about three or four months. And, as they worked their way back from the east coast, they came into Texas. It happened to be where his mom lived. Again, he had a meeting where very few people showed up. At this point, his head was kind of tucked between his legs and he was really frustrated. He showed up in his mom's house and his mom just says, "Why don't you go to take a nap?" So he takes a nap.

When he wakes up, he comes out to find this room full of 40 women that are over the age of 70 years old. Her mom happened to live in a retirement community, so she went around and gathered up all of her friends. She said, "Keith, they're here because they want to hear you speak. They want to hear what you have to say." And he's like, "Oh, these ladies don't want to hear what I have to say, Mom." And she says, "Well, yes they do."

So he starts presenting. And the way I presume it, he was selling and he was telling. He was out there and he started selling and telling people about this business. So she stopped him halfway through. She said, "Keith, tell them what you told me. Speak from your heart." So he put the presentation down and just started speaking from the heart about why he got in and what he wants to do with this. And all those ladies signed up that night.

It was probably more so because of his mom more than anything. But it gave him the courage to go on. And the analogy that he uses is, he says, "You know when I first got started, it was like I was sitting in a football stadium that seats maybe 50 thousand people and there was just me and my cousin. And about halfway through that year, my cousin decided to get out of the seat and leave." He decided to quit. He just said, "I can't take this anymore. I'm going back to Salt Lake. I'm going home."

But Keith continued on. After that meeting with his mom, he just continued on. And people started to show up a little bit more, little by little. By the end of the second year, he ended up with enough people in his organization to fill up a football stadium. By the end of the third year, he ended up with enough people in his organization to fill up a stadium twice. The moral of the story is that his cousin who got out of the seat, had he just stayed in his seat, would have been making over $200 thousand a month. But he got out of the seat. He wouldn't have to ever do anything had he just stayed in his seat.

That story resonates with me every time that I think about quitting or we've talked about quitting. Because you just never know and you just have to make the decision. Once you make the decision, you have to burn the bridges of retreat. There's no going back. Yes, it's the only option.

Doubt and disbelief is kind of like a cancer. A tiny little cancer cell gets inside your body and starts to fester and mature. And then it eventually starts to spread through your entire body. Doubt has the exact same effect. I mean, if you doubt even just the littlest bit, you won't succeed. Or, if you give yourself that option for plan B, so to speak, you will take it. No plan B.

Summer: But you know what, I think that's why it's so important to, like Travis said, burn the bridges. Don't have a plan B. Know that this is what you want. And you're going to have bad days, for sure. Expect that you will. I think you should have a plan for when you have a bad day, though. Something that you do that makes you feel good and will remind you of your goals. Maybe read a book or call your mentor, whatever it takes. Have a plan for the bad days. Never, no matter what, let that doubt creep in because you have to have confidence.

This kind of leads me to my next point, which is this: it's so crucial when you're getting started to surround yourself with the right people. Because you're going to have negative people; you have to avoid negativity like the plague. Seriously. I mean, you have to surround yourself with people who inspire and lift you up and believe in you. And, quite frankly, sometimes your family is the worst.

You remember the term "crabs in a bucket," right? This is where we see one crab try to crawl out and the rest pull it back down. A lot of times, people around you are comfortable with who you are now. They don't want to see you change. And so they're going to tell you you're going to fail. They're going to tell you you're crazy for thinking you can succeed. And with the first sign of failure, they're going to be all over you to tell you, "I told you this wouldn't work." And I think that if you're not surrounded with the right group of individuals, the right mentors, the coaches, you're not plugging in.

There's a saying in this industry that "Those who show up, move up." And what I mean by that is those who are on the calls, those that are coming to the meetings, those that are coming to the events, are surrounded by open-minded people. They're protecting their mind. It's like they're continually harvesting their mind. You either harvest weeds or you can harvest beautiful gardens, if you will. And it really depends on what you're allowing into your brain and your mind.

We are at a place in our life, where, if someone's negative, we don't want to talk to them. We don't want to be around them. We don't want to listen to them. If it's a negative person in our down-line, we, quite frankly, don't have time for that. We only have time for the individuals that have the same wishes and hopes and dreams and goals as we do.

And anybody else, you just have to have this straight and narrow path. And anybody else that deviates, you just have to avoid them. So, that would be something else I would share with someone who is a newbie.

Summer: And I think, too, that it's very important to have your spouse on board. There have been times when Travis is the lead in our business and, for him to be successful, I had to be supportive of him. Because there are times when he is away and the whole family can't go. A lot of times, we can bring our family, which is awesome. But there are times that the whole family can't go, or I can't go, and he has to work. If you have a supportive spouse, they will be happy and willing to make that sacrifice. Just know there are times when you have to sacrifice.

There is a saying: "Those that are willing to do today what others won't, will live tomorrow like others don't." So there are sacrifices that you have to make to continue to grow, continue to build, and to reach that next level, whatever that might be. When you have a negative spouse, it can destroy the business. We've seen it before. And they were these really blossoming, amazing entrepreneurs that were squelched by a negative spouse. Because they were like, "You know what? I don't want you to do this anymore." For that reason, I think that it's really important to make sure that the spouse is on board. And the way that you do that is by making them feel part of it and building a sense of community where you feel a part of that community.

It's not just the team of whoever it is; sometimes it is the woman who is to lead. So, that would apply the same to the man. But, I think that it's really important in a team to build a sense of community where both spouses feel like they're involved and feel like they're equally important. Because whichever spouse is the one that's staying home with the kids when the other one is out traveling or even staying home with a part-time job just to help financially until it builds up, that spouse is just as important.

And on those bad days, who are you going to be surrounded with? On those bad days we were talking about, that would be the time when an unsupportive spouse would say, "What? I told you I don't want you to do this. See, this wasn't a good idea." Or that spouse has the power to say, "You know what, baby, this is okay. It's just one day. I believe in you. I believe in us. I believe in our business. And I believe in our 'why,' our dreams. And you know what? This is just one bad day. Tomorrow is going to be amazing."

Well, you brought up a good point. Because Summer has done that for me in those times. I would say she's my secret weapon for a lot of different reasons. But apart from that, one of the biggest reasons is that she believes in me. You brought up a point, which is when you're a newbie, I can't tell you how important it is to find an organization that embraces the couple.

There are a lot of organizations that are primarily male-dominated. And, in some cases, it can be female-dominated as well. And although one may take the lead, I think that if you look at the ones that are the most successful people and emerging leaders today, they're power couples. They're couples that either work together or are just supportive of one another. It doesn't mean that they both have to be on stage. But they definitely are supportive of one another. One of the top reasons that someone will leave your organization is a negative spouse.

## Handling negativity

Having a negative spouse is indeed a difficult situation. What we have done to address that in our organization is to create a Women's Empowerment group that focuses on the women. We teach women how powerful they really are. And if they have a job or they are a full-time mom and they want to own a business at the same time, we teach them or help them to juggle those different things. We empower them with the life skills they need, essentially, to realize how powerful they are. I mean, women have power that we don't have. They absolutely do. And you look at this industry, 76% of the industry is women. And 80% of all the millionaires in the world that are women are in the direct sales industry. So, it's still a women-dominated industry.

What we've tried to do is really cater to the women and create a sense of belonging there. But going back to your question, the only thing that you can do is try to include them in everything. You just let them know that it's extremely important to you that they're on board with the decision that you're making. And it has to be a decision that's made together, ultimately.

Summer: Yes. I think that's probably where a lot of the negativity would come in — if the one spouse had made those decisions without including the other. So I think, getting started in the business, it's really important to make sure that that decision is made by both of them or that they were made to feel like it was both of their decisions and not just one.

I've seen a couple of marriages where it seems that they say that they're included, but really, a lot of the decisions are made by just one person. And I'm not saying that you have to. But just major decisions — travel decisions, the decision to be in the business, what's going on daily, include them in that. And I think that's where we've seen a lot of changes, when they have a spouse more included. There's more of a connection. Because a lot of times, people go to work for money in their daily jobs that are not in network marketing, and maybe the spouse works here and that one works there and they come home and they don't really want to talk about work sometimes. So I think it's a mind shift.

So, work is work. You come home. Home is home. That's why when you transpire that over into network marketing/direct sales, it's kind of the opposite. You want to be talking about work, when you go to work. But I think it can be a little bit of a shift in your mind sometimes. When you allow them to experience and share your experiences on a daily basis and talk about the growth of the business, I feel like that inclusiveness helps combat any negativity that could possibly come.

Even at the very beginning, a lot of people have said, "I want to join a business." They watch an opportunity meeting, then have to come home and explain it to their wife, who might be the negative spouse. I think it's important not to try to convince the wife or the husband to join the company. Don't convince them about the company. Convince them about the decision or why you want to be involved. Talk about the end game, the end result. Talk about the importance of time and being able to have the time and freedom to do the things that you want to do as opposed to the things that you have to do.

And get them on board with, ultimately, where you want to go — that financial freedom day first. Because once you get them on board with that, or once you get them to realize that what you're doing today is not going to get you to where you want to go, then it's much easier to say, "Well then, what are our options? Let's talk about some different vehicles." So for me, the financial freedom, always start with the goal defined.

Most people, I'd say, haven't taken the time to define where they want to go, right? So start at the end. Once you have a destination, it becomes much easier to analyze where you're at, and say, "What we're doing is not working. Let's talk about some options. And this is an option that I've recently come across that I think would be a good fit." This is more effective than coming in and saying, "Let me tell you about my product. Let me tell you about this juice. Let me tell you about this company I signed up for." That would be my advice to somebody who is a newbie with a negative spouse.

There's so much demand for couples being in business together. Bob Proctor, for example, has been asked the question, "What if my spouse is so negative and doesn't believe in all this self-development and financial freedom stuff and he or she just wants me to get a job?"

Summer: I think it goes back to the fact that even if I didn't believe in this product, I believe in him. And I want him to be happy. I want us to be happy. And I believe in our goals. And I believe in our dreams. And if that's the vehicle to help us get there, I don't think I necessarily have to care about the product. It's almost like, I care about him more. And I believe in him more. And I believe in our journey and where we're going together. You've just got to be on the same page about where you're going and that can make it so much easier.

## Lead generation

Here are some basics. The first one, and I'm going to talk about this today, is creating the party. Everywhere that you go, be the party. What I mean by that is, if we were to throw a party in our neighborhood and not invite a few of the neighbors, they're going to feel left out, right? Because we're having a party, people want to come. We throw fun parties.

Now, when you get involved in the industry, a lot of people are almost not proud of it and very quiet about it. They're not very confident about what they're doing. So what we teach is this: when someone calls you and asks how you're doing, the standard answer is "fine" or "okay."

What if the next time somebody called you and asked, "How are you doing?" you said, "You know what, it's really incredible! I opened myself up to some new opportunities recently and life is good! I can't even sleep at night. I'm so excited about the things that are going on in my life! 2011 for me, financially, is looking unbelievable! And I can't even tell you how excited I am!" What would they say? What do they do?

What I've just done is created posture, because the key to this business, in my opinion, is posture. If I called you up and said, "Hey, I've gotten into this new company! You've got to check this thing out. It's a pre-launch ground floor opportunity and great product! Let me tell you a little bit about the product. It's a blah-blah-blah product." And right away, you're going to put up a wall, because on a subconscious level, nobody wants to be sold. Everybody wants to buy, but nobody wants to be sold. So, on the other hand, what I just did in that little moment is have you come to me and I've created posture. And that's where most people go wrong in this business. They don't know how to create posture. They go out and, excuse the term, they "throw up on people."

You can create a party everywhere you go. Think about how many times a day people ask you, "Hey, how are you doing?" Think about Facebook, the different posts that you make. If I'm consistently positive and optimistic about what's going on in my life and enthusiastic, people can read that energy. They can feel your vibe. So, if you are constantly creating a party, bringing the party wherever you go, you're going to have leads. People are always going to want to know what you do.

Summer and I get emails, I'd say, once to twice a day, for people that we don't know in our social network. They say, "What are you doing? What do you do for a living? You're always so happy. I love your positive quotes." Or "I love your positive energy. I admire you for all of the inspiration that you give to other people." That's really complimentary to have someone come and reach out to you and you know that you affected their day.

So, bringing the party, creating the party, is the best thing that you can do. If the people that are close to you, your circle of influence, recognize the difference in you, they're going to ask you about it, whether it's the first day or the first week or the first month or first two months, they're eventually going to say, "What do you have going on?" because people are generally pretty miserable.

That means that 70% of all conversations are instinctively negative. That's 7 out of 10 conversations. The average child smiles, on average, between 400 to 500 times a day, while the average adult smiles 6 to 7 times a day. People are pretty miserable. So, when all of a sudden, they see you smiling, they're like, "What do you have going on?" So creating the party is the best way.

It serves two purposes — it creates leads and creates posture. People are going to come to you. You no longer pick up the phone and prospect incessantly. I'm not saying that there won't ever be a time where I have to pick up a phone and go out there and prospect. But this works really well. The second one, in our business, depends on your product, but most of the time, your product outflow is controlling your cash inflow.

If I'm in a business, it's a health and wellness business, I make a commitment to give out two to three samples a day. I'll go and hand out two or three of those samples a day or send out emails or hand them out to somebody. By the end of the month, that's 90 people. If I'm in business in my first month and I make a commitment to reach out, I call it "standing." Are you standing today? Did you talk with somebody, approach somebody about your business, or send somebody a product? If you're just sending out one or two samples, two to three samples a day, that's 30 to 60 people a month that you're putting in the process. You're going to find that out of those 30 to 60 people, 5 or 10 of them are either interested in learning more about your product or interested in learning how they can generate some income in your business.

The key to this business is consistent action, daily action. Managing your daily decisions and following through with those decisions daily. And, of course, that consistent action over a longer period of time will equal success. It's that consistency, it's the key. I hate to say that it's a numbers game, but the reality is this, you have to, as they say, "go for no." It is all about looking for your no's.

I'll share another story with you that I teach in residence with me. Picture a water ski. Have you waterskied before? Picture yourself behind the boat for your very first time. And that boat takes off, you're just starting to get out of the water and the boat stops. You sink right back into that water, right? The boat takes off again and then it stops and you sink again. Well, even if it's your first time, if you just keep going, you might crash a few times, it might hurt, but, if you keep doing it, eventually, you're going to get out of the water, you're going to start to gain a little bit of confidence, right? And then you're going to start to gain some momentum and, all of a sudden, there's no more resistance and you're gliding through the water. Now, you get a little bit more confidence and you cross the lake for the very first time, even though you might still be a little wobbly.

It's like when you do your first opportunity meeting or your first 3-way call. You're a little wobbly. But, pretty soon, you've done enough and you start jumping the lakes and all of a sudden, it's pretty simple. The key to that whole process is consistent action. And I think that, ultimately, daily activity, those daily actions, will lead to the confidence that will lead to the success. We're our own worst enemy.

## Daily routines

The first hour after I wake up, I won't take any calls. It's always personal growth, personal development time for me. I won't take a call until after 10:00 a.m. We get the kids off to school and generally, it's reading something, some type of a book, whatever book I'm reading at that time. After 10 o'clock then, I generally go down and check my emails and look at the most urgent calls for the day, start with those and kind of prioritize the day.

This is an area that I need a lot of work in personally. I don't have a structure in mind. But, I always start with my emails and calls that leads me usually into our leadership calls or our webinars that we do on a regular basis, opportunity webinars. And then, from there, I do whatever appointments that I have scheduled.

Usually, I start with my generals, my leaders, and contact them to find out what's going on in their business. I spend a lot of time building and promoting. I learned a long time ago that the top income earners know they've become expert promoters. They are always building for the next event. And, as a leader of our organization, I'm always promoting either Monday night's mentor call or Wednesday night's product call or Saturday morning's "getting started" call or the opportunity meeting that's going on Tuesday night. So, a lot of my time is taken by building and promoting and in organizing and structuring and all of those things.

For prospecting, I don't have a specific time, but I wouldn't suggest that structure. I find that I'm just not a structure kind of guy.

For somebody that's starting out as a newbie, I think that it's definitely a great idea to have a schedule of time when are you going to be prospecting. Make a decision as to how many calls that you are going to make and how many people you are going to reach out to and contact just beforehand.

I've gotten away from that, but what I've found is that we spend so much time working with our organization and working with our leaders and essentially running our organization that the prospecting comes more through talking with people and communicating with them or them contacting us on a weekly basis about our business.

When we first started, it was all about the calls. How many calls did we make? How many contacts did we make? How many at the end of each day, at the end of each week? I think it's great to have a daily activity log, a weekly activity log, and a monthly activity log. If somebody asks me or comes to me and says, "My business is not growing. What do I need to do? This is not working for me," the first thing that I'll ask them is this: "Are you willing to make a commitment to showing me what you do every single day?" Meaning, how many samples did you hand out? How many calls did you make? I want to know what your daily activity looks like, because you can usually track someone's success with their daily activities.

I gave him a daily activity sheet and at the end of the week, it adds up how many contacts that they made, 3-way calls they made, and samples they handed out, at the end of the month. And if they just make a commitment to do one to two of each one of those things each day, it's amazing how all of a sudden it adds up to 300, 400, or 500 exposures a month if you're being consistent with your actions. If not, it's very telling. So, for me, I think that somebody that's brand new, that's committed to do the business, should commit themselves to a daily and weekly tracker that tracks the things that are important for their company.

Summer: That's right. For us, though, we have a lot of success in decision making. And I know that that's not true for everybody, but, for us, it's very true. It's always been the daily activity.

## Using social media

We've had a lot of success with social media. There's a whole behavior and language and art to social media.

Summer: And we build our relationships through Facebook friends because it's more about relationship skills now. And it's always true. You attract people to you by what you put out. That's very true. And we've learned that.

## Personal development

The first book that I would start with is *The 17 Laws of Teamwork* by John C. Maxwell. I am big John Maxwell fan. *The 21 Irrefutable Laws of Leadership*, also by John C. Maxwell, will change your life. *How to Win Friends and Influence People* by Dale Carnegie is one of the top books that you need to pick up as well.

Actually, there are so many great books that are out there, but I think that those books right there are going to start working on the personal development and personal growth right away. *How to Win Friends and Influence People* is going to start to help people understand human behavior a little bit more. From the network marketing side of things, of course, you know, Big Al's book is always a great book. *My First Year in Network Marketing* is actually a very good book. *Developing the Leader Within You* is another great book by John C. Maxwell. *Think and Grow Rich* by Napoleon Hill is another phenomenal book for network marketers that are just getting started. I think those are all really good ones to start with and those would be at the top of my recommendation list.

## Mentors

Mentors change you. It is interesting because we had different mentors depending on the level where we were at. We look for people that inspire us and lift us up and motivate us and individuals that we want to be like.

Summer: We have to get along with them too. They have to be people that you like. Coaching and mentorship are two different things. You coach the masses, you mentor the few, and there is a relationship that is established with the direct mentor. There is a bond that's usually created in that situation, so it has to be someone that you trust enough to let them see who you are and that can be hard to do sometimes.

It's got to be somebody that you trust and that you know is going to take that trust and honor it. So that is something that we would look for, like-mindedness as far as personality. This is a business that you want to be around people that you enjoy working with. And I think the best predictor of the future or of future performance is past performance.

For us, we look at what people have accomplished in their lifetime and, ultimately, we have to accomplish what we have not and where we want to go. So those are all things that we take into consideration and that would be on a direct mentor level and indirect level. We all have a lot of indirect mentors like John Maxwell and Napoleon Hill.

## Masterminds

We have a mastermind call every Monday morning. That's my leadership or inner circle call which is with our generals. Outside of that, we don't. That was part of why we decided to come on this cruise, so we could get associated more with people outside of our inner circle. We feel like we are at a place in our career path, our journey, where we want to expose ourselves to other individuals are in another business and other industries and start to get more into the industry masterminding as opposed to just the inner circle masterminding within our team or our leaders. It is important, very important.

We have lots of personal friends that are leaders in other companies, actually within our neighborhood. We're fortunate that way, I think. We are able to keep our fingers on the pulse of the industry right in our own neighborhood by having lunch with others and talking about the industry as an informal mastermind.

Summer: And there are so many times that we, even just at our house at a barbecue with the neighborhood, we end up having conversations revolving around the industry, just because you know so many people that are big leaders in their perspective companies. Most of those leaders, I would say the majority of them, still have that attitude of "let's keep this quiet over here."

That is one of the things I am taking home from this trip is that sense of community and opening up to different companies in the industry and learning from their experiences.

## For beginners

I think it starts with daily steps and small steps; start with what you can manage. You know you are growing the most when you step outside of your comfort level. If you are afraid to speak in front of people, then perhaps you should start with an opportunity meeting or a 3-way call with your up-line. Find an opportunity where you might be able to share, even just sharing why you got into the business. Even that might be something that is uncomfortable for you, but your up-line should know where your comfort levels and boundaries are, so that they can include you in that process where you are comfortable.

When we bring somebody into the business, we can determine really quickly whether they are a duck or an eagle. We start them off in different places as far as where we'll include them into our system. Some, we put right into the conference calls, webinars, speaking on stage. That is not where we are going to start with them at all. Others have a comfort level to simply call someone and perhaps schedule an appointment and be the appointment setter for our presentation team to go and meet with someone. So, you've got to work with a newbie that is getting started, especially somebody who is an introvert, and help them find out where their comfort level is, then start with small baby steps.

For me, speaking is not a comfortable thing. I still get nervous when I speak in front of groups of people and I feel those nerves kick in. When

I first was asked to speak at a conference call and I was supposed to speak on a national call on Wednesday morning because of our success, I could not sleep from Sunday night to Wednesday. And all I had to do was a one to two minute little blurb about being on a phone call.

I did well enough on there that the diamond director came to me and said, "I want you to do the opportunity meeting on Wednesday night." And then I'm like, "Okay," but I am scared to death, right? So, the entire next week, I did not sleep and I was preparing and didn't sleep. Then they told me there were only 10 to 12 people there and 100 people showed up. And so I am sweating and shaking as I take a drink, but you have to take it in small steps.

My point is that a lot of this is about personal growth and you have to be willing to step outside that comfort level if you want to have success. If you are not growing, your business is not growing either. You've got to always be growing and be willing to step outside. I think it is important to take the pulse of where you are, what your comfort level is, and know and think about what that next step is for you, whether it would be to have an opportunity to speak on a conference call or introduce a meeting speaker who comes into town.

That was nerve-racking to me just to be able to introduce a big leader that was speaking. So all of those things are just tiny little steps moving in the right direction, moving forward and you just have to not take too much on your shoulders at once. Just take small steps and eventually speaking on a call will become easy. I know exactly where my comfort level threshold is right now and every time I go over it, I know that I am growing and feel that I am enjoying it.

Just speaking today, quite frankly, is a little bit nerve-racking for me. So is speaking in front of the leaders that I have looked up to for a long time who now, all of a sudden, I am speaking to. You know that got me alerted this morning. That is not a comfortable thing for me. It is exciting and I look forward to it. I know what I am going to talk about, but it is still something that makes my hands sweaty. That is just part of the growth. It is part of the business.

## What this business can do for you

I've got a GT1 Lamborghini watch. We kind of joke around, but we have a Lamborghini club on the boat. It is Jordan Adler, Todd Falcone, and myself. Jordan started this. He bought his watch the other day and I looked at and thought, "That's sharp." It just represents what the industry can do for you. I am a watch guy, so I saw Todd got one and that made me think about getting one even more. I kept looking at it and I kept thinking if I really want to buy it, even though it is not budgeted. I mean, it is something we can afford, but it is not something I would just go out and buy. I am not a spontaneous guy like that. When we went to look at it again, I noticed the last one was still there, and said, "I'll just buy it."

So I went ahead and bought it and it's a pretty cool watch. I'm pretty excited about it because it is just one of those things that I could not have imagined having seven years ago while we went through our trials. Now, we are on a cruise in the middle of the Caribbean and know exactly how much money we can spend. It is a pretty cool feeling.

To succeed, I think that there are two key crucial elements to that: being teachable and coachable. It's the first and most important part. People say they are teachable and coachable, but what does that mean, to be teachable and coachable? That means that you are willing to step outside of your comfort level. If you ask 10 people if they are teachable and coachable, nine of them will say "yes" but in reality, just two of them really are. So, if I bring somebody new into my business and I ask them, "Are you teachable and coachable?" and they say yes, then I expect them to do the things they need to do to succeed.

If there are things that they are not willing to do, well that is not really being teachable and coachable. We will never ask you to do something that is so far outside of your comfort level that you cannot handle or manage it, but, again, it comes back to that personal growth. Being teachable and coachable are number one for growth.

Number two, find a mentor. You must find a mentor and not just the mentor that you follow or someone you see onstage at a mastermind event. Find a mentor to work with intimately that is having the kind of success that you want to have and that you can see yourself working with on a regular basis. The thing that happens a lot is people think that it is the mentor's job to constantly be reaching out to the mentee. It's you who needs to be proactive.

People want me to mentor them and that is great. I am happy to mentor those individuals who are serious, but that means that the individual needs to really make an effort to be consistently communicating with me, letting me know what they are doing, what their challenges are, because there are these days where I am traveling or I might be gone or I just might be so overwhelmed.

Summer: Mentors are not mind readers, so if you're having a problem, then you need to call them because they may have no idea that you are going through this challenge and that you need help with this. You have to be able to have that open line of communication and feel comfortable reaching out to them and say, "Hey, this is what I need help with."

I work with you, I run with those who are ready to run, and I look to the people that are ready to run. Those people are constantly calling me, emailing me, are on the calls, and I can hear their voice; they are demanding my time. That's ultimately what you need to do if you really want a mentor. Be persistent, seek out a mentor or somebody who is having the success that you want to have and, ultimately, make a commitment to yourself and to that mentor that you're serious. Then, show them that you're serious. If you can avoid the pitfalls and trial and error that most people experience on their own just by aligning yourself with the right person, you will succeed much more quickly.

## Leaving a legacy

There's John Maxwell, who is probably the most influential person in my life from an indirect mentor's standpoint, who teaches that there are different levels of leadership. The highest level of leadership that one can obtain is the law of the legacy. When you hit that level, it's no longer about you or me anymore, it's about our ability to impact other people's lives, to make a difference, and truly live your legacy after you're gone.

And, just like financial freedom day, most people have not taken the time to find what that looks like. They don't take the time to define really what they want their legacy to be. Think of what you want your children to say about you after you're gone and what you want people to say about you. People haven't really taken the time to define that.

For us, legacy is about getting people to start thinking about what they want their legacy to be and then empowering them with the life skills that they need to start living their legacy. What we focus on is developing better husbands, better wives, and better community leaders. It's not just about the MLM. It's not about the product. It's not about the company. It's not even about the industry. For us, it's the cost that's much bigger than the industry. It's about going out and developing an army of leaders who can change the world. And part of living your legacy is changing the world through servant leadership.

If you look at the people who are the most memorable people, those who we view as leaders of our time, they understand a very important principle, and that is mentorship. You show me somebody who's extremely successful in life today, and I'll show you somebody who has a mentor, somebody who has someone that's leading them and guiding them. They have a team around them. Essentially, we believe in empowering people not only with those life skills that they need to start growing but also those skills that will help them grow their organization. The best way to grow an organization is to grow the people.

But also, part of living your legacy is being able to take control of your financial future. Money doesn't necessarily always leave a legacy. For some it will, but the freedom that money will give you will ultimately allow you to start shaping what you want your legacy to be.

For us, it's our children, it's our family, and it's the time that we spend together. This is the first trip that we've taken in a long time. If I have to go to California for a week and work, we take our children. And then, we go to Disneyland afterward. Then, on our way back, we stop at Vegas for a couple of days. So that's what we want our legacy to be. I want my children to say, "My Dad really was committed to his family. I remember all these moments and times we had together. He was focused externally on helping and changing others." You know what I mean? And that's part of what I want my legacy to be. The way that I'm going to live my legacy is through legacy. So, legacy, that's essentially what we are. We don't live with our company.

Legacy is an organization that we founded and we essentially talk more about legacy and explain how we've aligned ourselves with the home-based business opportunity that allows people to start taking control of their financial future. So, it's kind of a back-door approach to the industry — as opposed to going out and talking about my product and my comp plan and all these things. I'm talking about something that truly resonates. That's legacy.

We're actually at a point in our group staff where Legacy has been received so well that we've had a lot of people from other companies approaching us saying they just want to be a part of that. But, right now, our income stream is solely from the organization in the down-line.

We are in the process of writing this book and releasing this book. It's the first step in launching "Legacy." I'm not sure what the title will be yet, but it will be something about legacy life coaching and it will be outside of the Legacy organization. It will be outside of the industry. It will be more so about the same mission and will be available to anybody inside or outside the industry. Then, ultimately, one step is that everybody will have somebody in their life as a mentor. So we are working on that right now.

Summer: When we started, we had only decided what we didn't want. We knew want we wanted when we were at that phase and we knew we had to do something.

We decided to look forward to what we wanted. And I think that has to do with deciding what our "why" was, but also think a lot of it had to do with what we wanted our legacy to be, where we wanted to go, and the journey that we wanted to take. And that was a huge pivotal moment where we decided not to give up because that didn't match where we wanted to go.

Live up to your legacy by taking control of your life. It will ultimately define what you want your legacy to be. Then start living up to it.

— Summer & Travis Flahtery

# FROM ZERO TO MILLIONS STRATEGY

- Find yourself a mentor who you trust and believe in.
- Define what you want your legacy to be and start living up to it.
- Associate yourself with positive, like-minded people.
- Create the Party.
- Be teachable and coachable.
- Establish relationships.
- This business is about growing yourself as a leader.
- This business is about helping people go from where they are today to where it is that they want to be.
- No plan B
- Are you "standing"?
- Utilize your time by planning your calls and sponsoring.
- Keep track of your activities.
- Leaders are followers.
- Get out of your comfort zone, the only way to grow, read, and be the best you can be.

# SUGGESTED RESOURCES

Resources to help you achieve your wildest dreams

*The 17 Laws of Teamwork* by John C. Maxwell
*The 21 Irrefutable Laws of Leadership* by John C. Maxwell
*How to Win Friends and Influence People* by Dale Carnegie
*Big Al Tells All* by Tom Big Al Schreiter
*My First Year in Network Marketing* by Mark Yarnell
*Developing the Leader Within You* by John C. Maxwell
*Think and Grow Rich* by Napoleon Hill
*Rich Dad Poor Dad* by Robert Kiyosaki
*Secrets of the Millionaire Mind* by T. Harv Eker
*The Outlier* by Malcolm Gladwell
*Influence* by Robert B. Cialdini
*The Power of Positive Thinking* by Norman Vincent Peale
*The Million Dollar Tip* by Andrew Carnegie
*The Magic of Thinking Big* by David J. Schwartz
*The Law of Attraction* by Esther & Jerry Hicks
*How to Get Rich* by Felix Dennis
*The Slight Edge* by Jeff Olson
*The Richest Man in Babylon* by George S. Clason
*The Speed of Trust* by Steven M. R. Covey

CD — "Building Your Network Marketing and Business" by Jim Rohn
CD — "The First Year in Network Marketing" by Jim Rohn
CD — "The Simple Art of Duplication" by Art Jonak
CD — "How to Be a No-Limit Person" by Wayne Dyer

# ABOUT THE AUTHOR

**WHO I am and what I do:** I am an architect, artist, coach, entrepreneur, author, and upcoming speaker. Born in the country 40 miles west of Copenhagen, Denmark into a farming family, I learned right from early childhood to work and help out. I learned the meaning of responsibility early on which taught me to be helpful and thankful for the lesson learned later in life.

As a "blue personality colour" (according to Tom "Big Al" Schreiter's personality colours), I always wanted to see the world. I had restlessness inside of me and was eager to explore. As the famous Danish writer Hans Christian Andersen said, "To travel is to live." I have done exactly that. I have lived in France, Spain, England, the United States of America, Turkey, Romania, Croatia, Sweden, and, of course, Denmark. I have travelled to more than 50 countries so far.

I began my career in construction management and design working on various multi-scale projects from Russia to Asia. Later in my life, I took an MA in Architecture and worked for worldwide corporations as an expert consultant.

Consulting for The European Union working on construction projects founded by the investment bank. Developing and constructing education facilities which helped millions of young girls and their families have the ability to educate themselves with the same opportunity boys have in eastern Turkey and northern Romania. Education possibilities have always been only for boys, an old culture pattern that is now gradually changing.

I decided at the height of my career to make a change. I was designing and building buildings for people, but I wanted to instead "build

221

people." I got hooked on personal development and did a documentary film in six episodes about coaching. The film focused on how we can become more conscious about our belief system and take control over our own lives. We should be aware of how our habits and paradigms are controlling us and stop those habits in order to procure a better life.

I grew up in a culture and environment with old, traditional ways of thinking about making money. As I started to expand my awareness, I studied the principle of creating MSI (multiple sources of income). I was pleased to meet Bob Proctor and study his materials and programs. He really opened my mind and increased my awareness.

Shortly after, I was introduced to direct sales and had some success, but nothing substantial. I made a big mistake, which was expecting my down-line to start performing. As you will read in my book, this is a common mistake. I decided to look for answers about how to maintain and build a successful and sustainable down-line. As a very curious person always hungry for answers, I started asking myself questions that I knew somebody in the network marketing industry could answer. Because success leaves clues. I then started focusing on finding a common forum where I could get my questions answered.

As a result of that search, I got into contact with 11 top-notch earners from different direct sales companies, who shared their amazing stories of how they succeeded in their business. I was so overwhelmed with all the knowledge I learned from these interviews that I decided to turn it into a book, helping other "hungry" people who were searching for the same answers I was.

**MY vision in life:** My vision is to inspire others and be the best I can be. I desire to motivate others to really discover their dreams and start taking action steps to achieve them.

**My home, social life, passions, and leisure:** At the moment, I live in Malmoe, Sweden, a city with more than 120 languages spoken. Malmoe is a mecca for artistic, creative people and just a short distance from Copenhagen, Denmark. It is a great location. You can travel just across the bridge and 20 minutes later, you are in the center of Copenhagen. Or you can travel 12 minutes by train, and you're right at the airport connecting to various European or worldwide destinations.

**Social Life:** I am unmarried, but did get very close to marrying in Turkey. However, my restless soul wanted to move on to explore new adventures. My logical brain won instead of my heart. I've met beautiful women around the world and enjoyed dating and hanging out. I love being around open-minded, high-energy people that can inspire me and challenge my beliefs.

**Passions:** Since childhood painting and drawing have always been my passion. I drew a lot as kid - most kids do until they get tired of hearing mom and grandma yelling that they have to stay in the lines. But as I entered my teens, I got into music, sports, and all of the other teenage hair-raisers. I didn't quit painting; I just never got around to it. Through my professional life as an architect, I have always been connected to art. But it wasn't until later in life in Ankara, Turkey that my eager desire to express myself came to life.

I have donated some paintings to schools in Romania while working and living in there. I've also exhibited some in different places in Denmark and Europe. The events in my life, the laughter with worthwhile people, good music, songs, challenges, are all reflected in my paintings. The artwork may have nothing to do with the event, but every painting is charged with the emotions of the time. It's like hearing that certain song come on the radio and BOOM - you're right back in high school with a broken heart.

I don't see the subject in my paintings, really. I'm pulled back into what was happening in my life at the time I painted it. It demonstrates how art and life are inseparably linked. When art 'clicks,' that means it triggered an emotional response (http://noelluis.deviantart.com/gallery). If the art has enough of that 'something' to spark smiles and memories, there's a real connection between art, artist, and viewer.

And THAT is why I do what I do, giving the audience an unforgettable experience with a high level of energy and a reflection for the mind, soul, and imagination. And to go to the lengths that I go, people only respond to passion, authenticity and the authority of experience. Recently I got together with Nadia Russ in a catalogue published called 21st Century ART http://books.google.com/books/about/Neopoprealism_Starz.html?id=DBF4HQYhPmIC.

I also play instrumental music which I have composed, and my music recordings have brought joy to many people in Denmark. I just love the sound of the saxophone mixed with modern rhythms. My music comes intuitively to me from within.

"Feel it and keep moving, because you deserve to be happy."
— Rainer Maria Rilke

**Leisure:** I am a mountain biking enthusiast, hiker, scuba diver. I adore all kinds of outdoor activities. I also love artwork, photography, investing, psychology, feng shui, interior design, architecture, graphic design, reading, studying personal development, leadership, and communication.

Dedicated to your success,
Noel Luis

"Thinking, writing, and speaking of the future is a way to bring your dreams to life."
— Dave Ellis

www.ingramcontent.com/pod-product-compliance
Lightning Source LLC
Chambersburg PA
CBHW021400210526
45463CB00001B/170